WILLY RUSSELL AND HIS PLAYS

Table of Contents

ACKNOWLEDGMENTS

I wish to thank Willy Russell for his great contribution to this book. Michael and Margaret Seagroatt kindly let me borrow their collection of material on Willy Russell and made detailed criticism of the first draft. However, any mistakes in this book are entirely my own responsibility.

I am grateful to the Leverhulme Trust Research Awards Advisory Committee for awarding me grants in 1987 and 1988 to work on this project. The book arose from W.E.A. courses I taught in Liverpool from 1985 to 1989 on the plays of Willy Russell and my thanks go to the W.E.A. and my students.

Several other people also gave me valuable help: Anna Davidson, Spencer Leigh of BBC Radio Merseyside, Jerry Dawson of Unity Theatre, Liverpool, John Tagholm of Thames Television, Andy Melia, Tony While and Bernard Draper. Miss J.Wright typed out my manuscript, Mrs Beryl Hunwick audio-typed the interview, Mrs Lillie Wilmot word-processed the book, and Mr C.D.Price gave advice. I also want to thank my wife Heather for critical advice and my parents for their support.

References from 'Blood Brothers' and'Lies' are by permission of Willy Russell and Casarotto Ramsay Limited; references from 'Shirley Valentine' are by permission of Willy Russell and Methuen London.

LIST OF ILLUSTRATIONS

(Copyright <u>Liverpool Daily Post and Echo</u> unless otherwise stated)

Willy Russell at rehearsals for 'Shirley Valentine' at the Vaudeville, London. (Catherine Ashmore)

LIST OF PLAYS BY WILLY RUSSELL

1. Stageplays

'Keep Your Eyes Down' (1971)
'Blind Scouse': 'Keep Your Eyes Down', 'Playground' and 'Sam O'Shanker' (1972)
'The Tale of Blind Joe McSweeney' in 'The Cantril Tales' (1974)
'Breezeblock Park' (1975)
'One For the Road' (1976-79)
'Stags and Hens' (1978)
'Educating Rita' (1980)
'Blood Brothers' (1981)
'Shirley Valentine' (1986)

2. Musical Plays

'When The Reds' (1973)
'Sam O'Shanker' (1973)
'John, Paul, George, Ringo ... and Bert' (1974)
'Blood Brothers' (1983)
'Our Day Out' (1983)

3. T.V. Plays

'King of The Castle' (1973)
'The Death of a Young, Young Man' (1975)
'Break In' (1975)
'Lies' Parts I & II (1977)
'Our Day Out' (1977)
'Daughters of Albion' (1979)
'The Boy with the Transistor Radio' (1979)
'Politics and Terror' (1980)
'One Summer' (1984)
'Terraces' (1993)

4. Screenplays

'Educating Rita' (1983)
'Shirley Valentine' (1987)
'Dancin' thru the Dark' (1989)

5. Radio Plays

'I read the news today' (1976)

6. Unfinished or Professionally Unproduced Plays

'Breakdown'
'The Bent'
'Lucy Wan'
'Playmates'
'Man Who Killed the Motor Car'
'Point Eight'
'Tam Lin'
'Screwed Down'
'John, Paul, George, Ringo...and Bert' (Screenplay)
'Band on the Run' (Screenplay)
'On the Rob' (with Alan Bleasdale)
'Sculliver's Travels' (with Alan Bleasdale)

INTERVIEW WITH WILLY RUSSELL

J.G. Do you feel Liverpool is a stimulus for you? Or do you have mixed feelings about Liverpool in that for certain people it's a bad place to live because of the inner city as a place of decay with the collapse of industry?

W.R. No, I am not singling out Liverpool, I just happen to write in Liverpool but I use Liverpool as a metaphor for wherever. I know it's the same in Bradford, I know it's the same in Barnsley, I know it's the same in Glasgow and Newcastle. All right, they have geographical, regional, idiomatic differences, but the stories I tell set in Liverpool are stories that happen in other languages in Bradford, Burnley, Glasgow and Newcastle, but that said, yes, there is something absolutely particular about Liverpool because of the nature of the idiom here. It is a wonderful language for somebody who

Willy Russell outside the Everyman Theatre in 1986.
(Phil Cutts)

works in the spoken form, and ultimately that is what I do, I write words which will only come into their own when they are spoken on a stage, during an engagement with an audience. Now, if I had been born in Crewe, Shrewsbury or where ever, the chances are I would not be a dramatist, I may have become a novelist, a poet, but not a dramatist because in Crewe and in Shrewsbury and Ashby de la Zouche, there is not the strongly defined language in the first place and there is not a people who've always been rather extrovert in their linguistic behaviour, creative in their linguistic behaviour and fundamentally proud of that behaviour, that language. I remember when I was a kid, getting off a boat in the Isle of Man and somebody said 'Where do you come from?' and 300 kids go 'Liverpool'. Now the kids from Crewe weren't saying 'Crewe', or 'Ashby de la Zouche' - there is this sort of ridiculous pride and not only the pride, but the bottle to say it. The arrogance, if you like, to say 'Liverpool' so, whilst I

9

don't think about it consciously, I can unselfconsciously bring all that to bear on my work. I do like to revel in the language but not in some of the blinkered attitudes that go along with that language. Yet, in almost all of the plays you will find there is a significant character who speaks without accent. Mrs Kay in 'Our Day Out', Kidder in 'One Summer', Frank in 'Rita', Eddie and the Lyons family in 'Blood Brothers', Marjorie Majors in 'Shirley Valentine' and also many others. So that the plays are not purely idiomatic of Liverpool because I do not want to write plays that only make sense in Liverpool, I am not interested in stroking that rather blinkered 'we are Scousers' attitude. One of the things worth noting is, of course, that before Alan Bleasdale and I began to work in this accent, it was not approved of, it was not accepted as a dramatic conduit. It could be used by comedians, but poets didn't use it. When you think back Roger McGough, Brian Patten and Adrian Henri didn't use this idiom, because in poetic circles they would have been accused of being merely regional, idiomatic, dialect writers. It is fascinating that in the last ten or fifteen years, the poets have used the language more and more but previously they didn't. Robert Burns suffered from that. Critics of the day scoffed at the fact that he wrote in a Scottish idiom. There is still that sort of blinkered attitude. It is interesting reading Joe Orton's diaries in which he picks up a play by David Rudkin and pours scorn on it because it is written in dialect. He had this rather sniffy, metropolitan attitude towards anyone who worked in an idiomatic language. Now, prior to Alan and I working in this language, the only thing you could do in Liverpudlian was be funny. Peter Maloney and Arthur Dooley would be on TV. Certainly, when local radio began, nobody but nobody spoke in a Liverpool accent and you certainly didn't have commercials on TV that used Liverpool accents. So, for me one of the big revelations was when I watched John McGrath's work at the Everyman. Although prior to that in the folk song clubs, I had been working in accents. I'd seen other people do it, principally Tony Murphy, who had written some songs for the Spinners to record, like 'The Orange and the Green', and then I discovered Peter McGovern and he was writing in this idiom, and the wonderful songwriter Stan Kelly who wrote 'Liverpool Lullaby'.

Now, before ever going near a theatre, I discovered that regional accents, idiomatic languages, weren't just to be paraded as something odd or funny, because here were people like McGovern and Murphy who were writing ostensibly comic songs but songs which did have a serious impact and Stan Kelly was often writing very harrowing material. I am thinking of 'Liverpool Lullaby' particularly, it is a beautiful piece of work, and it connects with ballads going back 700 years. All they were doing was continuing the tradition because it was a self-conscious socialist movement working in the language of working people. So before I ever came to the theatre, I was very used to that. But, when I first came into the theatre, I thought that you didn't work in those languages; you did in T.V. plays but not in drama at the theatre, and it was only through seeing McGrath's 'Unruly Elements' and later, 'Fish in the Sea', that I

10

discovered I could work in this language in the theatre.

J.G.   So that was a really important turning point for you, going to the Everyman that particular evening in 1971 and seeing McGrath's 'Unruly Elements'?

W.R.   It was a turning point, but it must be seen in the context of everything else that was happening up to that time. Don't forget that before seeing that I had read James Reeves' Idiom of the People; I was seriously engaged with the idea of language, with the idea that in Britain, as in most countries, there is one language for high art and there is folk and street art which don't use that same language. It would have to be mediated into art language, just as the composers have done endlessly. Vaughan Williams would hear a Suffolk singer singing, say, 'The Seeds of Love', would note the beauty of the tune but would not present the tune in all its sensational, noble beauty. He probably couldn't have done, he would have to mediate it into an acceptable art language 'worthy' of the concert platform. Bela Bartok did the same thing. Many composers based their music on traditional music, but didn't present it in that way. Now, I was part of the movement that was anti that and was trying to say: no - don't mediate it, it doesn't need to be mediated. What we have to try and do is confront the question of the two languages, of the art language and the street language.

Willy Russell in his office in Liverpool, 1990.
(Matthews Woodland)

J.G.   Is this an oral tradition?

W.R.   Yes, a sort of non-approved language, that is still worthy of doing great things.

J.G.   Is that one way of looking at 'Educating Rita' - the formal language used by academics as against the street language used by someone who is untutored in that kind of language?

W.R.   Even though I am using them here, I would be very careful using phrases like 'street language' and 'folk language' because they are terribly misleading, and the fact is that Rita is extraordinary in her use of language anyway, so that if you saw Rita in her own milieu you would see that she is extraordinary just as Shirley Valentine is extraordinary. They don't live their lives thinking 'I am

11

extraordinary', but they would be two women who would dominate a group of women always, because of their language.

J.G.   And do you see this oral tradition emerging from the working class or is it a more general stream of communication? Is it strong in Liverpool and particularly strong among women?

W.R.   No, not only in Liverpool, it is also extremely strong in Scotland, the North East and Yorkshire, but it tends to have remained strong in the working class areas. Because, don't forget, that in historical terms it is extremely recently that the working classes have had literature imposed on them. The first Education Act was only yesterday, in historical terms and so we have a situation in which oracy is still the primary mode of communication. I am not saying that oracy is purely the preserve of the working class, but that most of the working class culture, conventions, codes of behaviour have been carried and passed on orally, whereas middle class culture is largely a literary culture.

J.G.   In theatrical terms, this was very much generated by the Everyman under Alan Dossor, wasn't it?

W.R.   Alan Dossor was coming from elsewhere. Alan had no particular knowledge of this folk song movement but in his way, theatrically what he was trying to do was to break down the arts stranglehold which was middle-class dominated. He wanted to see a theatre which related to the people in whose town it operated. So we were obviously both moving towards the same point; Dossor was an educated, university man, I wasn't. He himself would almost be mediated into a middle class position in the role of director but our instincts were the same, though we couldn't have articulated it, and McGrath, of course, was coming at things from the same way.

J.G.   And that was a very exciting period at the Everyman, in 1973 wasn't it?

W.R.   It was phenomenally exciting, because it was my first professional work. It was dizzying. I would walk into the theatre and the company would walk in and I'd be sitting down, having breakfast and discussing notes with Jonathan Price, George Costigan, Julie Walters, Anthony Sher, Bernard Hill, Liz Estensen, Philip Joseph and Trevor Eve, but we didn't sit there thinking 'My God - we are making history', and God help us if we had've done. We were just struggling young workers having a crack at where we thought it should be. In those days I was at college and I used to go to the library every month to get hold of <u>Theatre Quarterly</u> and I remember reading a long interview with Christopher Hampton, who was then about 30 and who had had two plays in the West End. I remember sitting there thinking 'It was really interesting that, well I will probably write a West End play when I am 30, but now I am involved in a completely different type of theatre.'

12

J.G.   And you don't like to see yourself, narrowly as a Liverpool playwright or a West End playwright? You are happier to see yourself in terms of being a playwright?

W.R.   Well, yes, one of the significant things is that when I wrote 'John, Paul, George, Ringo ... and Bert', I said to Alan Dossor, I have got two ideas of how to approach this, one is a play which would completely observe the unity of time and space and one is a play that would be written in the Everyman house style, which do you want? And rather disappointingly for me at the time, he said 'I want one in the Everyman house style'. Disappointing because (a) I sensed that the Everyman house style of those days was in danger of becoming a formula and (b) because I wanted to demonstrate that I could handle other, more traditional forms of theatre. I soon came to realise though, that Alan Dossor was right. In terms of a story about The Beatles, his instinct regarding the appropriate style was much better than mine and once I began to write the play I was far from disappointed. Nevertheless, I did still have a hankering to write a drama along more well known lines.

J.G.   Were you tempted to do another pop music piece after the success of 'John, Paul, George, Ringo ... and Bert'?

W.R.   'Breezeblock Park' followed on because I still wanted to go to the opposite end of the spectrum, to show that I could do something very different from 'John, Paul, George, Ringo ... and Bert'. I was flooded with requests to do the Rolling Stones story, but I'd done it, I'd gained my satisfaction from it. Now, if I had written 'John, Paul, George, Ringo ... and Bert' and it had only run for three weeks at the Everyman, and not many people had seen it, maybe a couple of years later I would have tried it again because I would have been trying to get it right, but I know I got it right the first time. You walked into the preview at the theatre and you just knew it was right. So I couldn't repeat that but, obviously, to leap forward 10 years or so, I did go back to that style, and used the best of it and acknowledged, in a sense, the training I had received in that style in 'Blood Brothers', which was firmly written in that Everyman

Willy Russell in his office in Liverpool. (Matthews Woodland)

13

style, although it opened at the Playhouse. And, my description of the style is, I suppose, one that takes its springboard more from the cinematic than theatrical writers. You write in scenes - it is not classicist, it is not even neo-classicist, you can break the rules, you can cover a few years, you can have a large cast played by eight people doubling, you can move locations, you don't have to say we're now moving from this room to the next room, we can go from Mount Etna to just across the High Street. That is the style and it has only just occurred to me now that one of the things that Dossor was doing was to try and bring us Brecht shot through with Joan Littlewood.

J.G.   You have had a lot of academic training yourself, so you are combining various streams, aren't you? You have the academic input and you have that folk music stream flowing in as well. I mean you had that for six years.

W.R.   You know the crude bio of Willy Russell is, he left school with no 'O' levels, became a ladies' hairdresser, walked into a theatre and became a playwright. I mean that is bullshit. There have been attempts to document what I have done in the theatre and why I write in the style that I do, but it does not take into account the fact of years spent thrashing about in earnest debate, debate the likes of which you can only ever know if you are part of one of those zealous revivalist movements like the folk song movement. I had the great good fortune during those years to come into contact with some of the best writers, some of the wisest people, like Bert Lloyd, probably the greatest of the folk artists, a folk song expert, a great man, who never functioned as an academic, and I met him because he came to sing at festivals. He was a massively self-educated man, extremely wise. I was sitting at dinner once with Michael Seagroatt. Now Michael is a 70-year-old authority on European films and Bert started talking about films and it was just fascinating to see the two of them together. Bert has the most fantastic spread of film experience. A lot of people in the folk song movement were in it purely because they couldn't function anywhere else. Now this wasn't true of Bert. He was a broadcaster, singer, collector, composer, he worked in films, he worked in theatre and folk song was just one of his interests. I was able to meet people like Ewan McColl, Charles Parker, Phillip Donnellan and Christie Moore, so I met with the best brains in that movement, and I was able to either discuss with them or be in situations where I heard them debating this question of an art that was not recognised as a high art form, that they felt did not need to be mediated into a palatable middle class mode. I would listen to Charles Parker describing how he recorded a woman on the fish quays at Aberdeen and he would play us some of her unselfconscious language that was high-flown poetry. It didn't need to be apologised for. Because I had been a writer on this folk scene, I had flirted with the idea of trying to write something dramatic, that could be staged at festivals. But there's a terrible self-defeating folksiness about the folk-song movement. Its ultimate paradox is that the movement that was being run by socialists was deeply conservative, as often socialism is, and so the folk movement was locked back in the 19th century,

Willy Russell in his office in Liverpool.
(Matthews Woodland)

back in rural Britain, because it sang largely rural ballads. Now, to go back to the best of these people, they weren't merely reviving the past. Charles Parker could see a connection between a 17th century ballad collected by Francis J. Child about Sir Patrick Spense and a woman in a shopping mall, because he knew that both lives were capable of mythic, epic interpretation, a perspective. I knew I could write and communicate but I couldn't find a platform within that movement to do it because of its conservatism, and by happy accident discovered that I could do it within the theatre.

J.G.   The folk singing period in your career lasted from 1965 to 1972 didn't it? You were very dedicated to it, as you have just been saying. During this period you were hairdressing, and you were folk singing on a semi-professional basis and getting a reasonable living. Was that the general picture at that time?

W.R.   Yes, in and around Liverpool then you had 30 clubs, so I would spend most nights of the week with other musicians, playing sessions or within folk clubs because I was receiving a great education as well as anything else and, as Art with a capital 'A' held nothing for me at that time, I did need some sort of sustenance. I found it in discovering the whole body of music that was nothing to do with high art and yet was enriching.

J.G.   Let's take the discussion back a little in time, in terms of looking at why women are important in your plays. Is it too simple to say it is because you regard women as having a language of their own, a language that discusses human emotions whereas men feel very uncomfortable about discussing such matters?

W.R.   Yes - it is simplistic and I only say that when I am put on the spot. Because I can't truly find a reason as to why I should write about women. All I can do is look at my own past and, just as any other observer, I can try to find clues as to why it is. You've got to understand that a lot of what anyone does as a writer, is pure instinct. You can't shut instinct up, because if you do you're dead. Who knows, when writing 'Educating Rita,' perhaps I instinctively felt that it would stand more chance as a play because it was a hefty part for a woman and there weren't many big parts for women. I don't think so, because I don't

15

think I am that calculating even instinctively or unconsciously. But there might have been an element of calculating that the play would have more impact with a woman, rather than a man at its centre.

J.G. Can we talk about the women in your life? Going back to your childhood, your Dad was out working for I.C.I. and you were brought up by your mother, your grandmother and your Auntie Dorothy, and so you were mainly in the company of women.

W.R. I was often in the company of women, and don't forget it was a very tightly-contained housing estate.

J.G. Knowsley Village, before it became a massive borough?

W.R. That's right. It's knocked down now. It was a whole group of houses that were built for R.A.F. munitions workers during the war. It was plonked down in the middle of fields so what you had was a sort of urban capsule in the middle of this rural paradise. And most of my references when I was brought up were rural. But I had an urban language, as all the people who lived out there came from a town, but I used to go literally from my house to across the street and I was pea-picking. I spent most of my time in the woods and around streams. Lord Derby's estate was all around us and don't forget this wasn't an estate where the motor car connected us because nobody could afford one. So on that estate there were my parents, my Auntie Dolly, my grandmother, who ran a mobile grocers; my other relatives lived nearby. These girls, like my mother and Dolly and Edna still gravitated to their mother. She was still boss, so I suppose that was one of the ways in which one was able to see life from this somewhat female perspective.

J.G. And there was a great deal of conversation going on in your presence?

W.R. I suspect so, yes, and I think I must have unconsciously been privy to the women's view of the world. Remember at this time, just after the war, most of the men were in full employment and out, away from the house, working shifts.

J.G. Your parents loved books and storytelling and you loved reading at a very early age didn't you? I remember you said you would curl up by the fire and find friendship in a book.

W.R. It was a terribly sensual thing to do, to lie down by the fire with a bag of sweets and a book. I mean, it really was womb-like. Certainly, I always associated books with complete and utter happiness and safety and security.

J.G. Well, we have got to link that directly with the experience you have written

16

about in a preface to your plays, when you describe an experience at secondary school in a quiet reading period with the sun streaming through, you are reading a novel and this was another major turning point when you sensed, wouldn't it be marvellous to be a writer, to create in people the feeling that you had experienced. Is it fair to say that was an important experience, sitting there in the class, in Rainford High School?

W.R. Yes, but it was also pretty important at age 7 or 8, standing up in class and reading my story out and knowing that it hit the nail on the head, it got laughs where it needed to get laughs and it engaged people. Whereas the rest of the people in the class would go 'the dog sat on the mat', I could see that that was naff, because if you were reading a story out, you had to grab the listener. I knew at that precocious age, I wasn't precocious about it, I wasn't always writing stories, badgering people to listen to them. But I knew I could do it well. It was the only thing I knew I could do well, I could play football but I knew I was never going to be a great football player. Later on I could play a guitar but I knew I was never going to be a great guitarist. I can write a line of prose, I can write a line of verse, but I am not an expert. I am an expert dramatist. I know when I look at a play of mine, why it works, where it does work and where it doesn't work. I am not an expert when I am fumbling to write the next one. But once I am on it, I am ruthless in applying that expertise to the job of writing, because I know it and I cannot busk hoping something will stick, something will somehow just fall right.

J.G. So how long does that writing period take? I expect there isn't a set time, it depends on the nature of the play and how much time you need to take.

Willy Russell in his office in Liverpool.
(Matthews Woodland)

W.R. You can't look at it in hourly terms, can you. It is impossible. With 'Blood Brothers', I gave myself three months in which to write the musical and of course, I found I couldn't. It was hopeless rushing to try to write a musical, so it took me twelve months. Now, fortunately I was working for Chris Bond at the time, who is, being a writer himself, a very flexible director, so when 'Blood Brothers' was supposed to open but wasn't ready he drafted in a revival

17

of 'Breezeblock Park', and then found another play until it could open. It was the only time that has ever happened to me and I didn't feel that I was letting anybody down because I genuinely had warned him of the situation. I knew that if I cobbled together something in three months it wouldn't have worked - it would require a lot more time but, normally, I will set aside 3 - 6 months in which to do it.

J.G.   I know you have only written one radio play - 'I Read the News Today'. Is that because you have only had one commission?

W.R.   No, I have had lots of people trying to commission me for radio, the problem is - how can I say this without sounding sneering towards a medium of which I am extremely fond? I suppose the fact is that I feel that, if I can write a good 90-minute radio play, I have actually got a good 90-minute film or stage play. If radio was at the centre of our culture as it was 40 years ago I would be undoubtedly writing for radio but, sadly, radio is marginalised now, and my instinct is always to work at the centre. I know that some people will say that the theatre is not the white-hot centre but I can't agree with that.

J.G.   Was your own family at all theatrical?

W.R.   I wasn't aware of this at the time but now, looking back, even though I or they never spent time in the theatre I had been brought up by a very theatrical family, theatrical in an unselfconscious sense, a family that was very fond of stories in one form or another. A member of the family would tell you about being somewhere on a Saturday night, and they would tell it in such a way that it had dramatic impact. So unbeknown to me, I had had a sort of informal training.

J.G.   When did you become conscious of theatre?

W.R.   I think truly my first experience of theatre was on the back of a motor bike with a then friend of mine who was driving this bike. He went to the theatre occasionally and he started to tell me about the play that he had seen that week, which was 'Romeo and Juliet'. He told me the story and I thought it was a devastating, sensational story but I probably thought of it as a film, rather than as a play. I certainly would never have thought 'well, I shall now go to a theatre.' It was something that this odd-ball mate of mine could do but I wouldn't go. That was the first time that I became aware of theatre, albeit without going into one. Then I saw a couple of amateur productions when I was about 19; one was some potboiler and one was 'The Importance of Being Earnest' but again I didn't relate to this experience other than to mildly enjoy it. Because I was going out with somebody who went to the theatre as a matter of course, I saw a lot of the work of Unity, most of which was rather poor and it didn't engage me, it seemed largely rather irrelevant to me. And I saw some bits at the Playhouse which again seemed terribly remote, they were awful

18

really, and it was only seeing McGrath's work at the Everyman that made theatre something highly accessible and directly relevant.

J.G.   And you were soon writing for the Everyman.

W.R.   I'd done an adaptation and a small-scale touring play. Then, in December '73 I began work on the play about The Beatles. It wasn't so much a turning point as an earthquake. The whole of my life changed because of it. I was commissioned to write a play which would have normally run for three weeks in a 400 seat theatre and it ended up running for over a year in a 1,000 seat

The 'Kirkby Town Three', Derek Edwards, Dave Bell and Willy Russell (right) at Granada T.V. in 1967. (Granada T.V.)

theatre in the West End of London. Now when that happens, your life changes. It was a funny situation. At the time it was terrifying to write a play about The Beatles in Liverpool. Because, as you know, there were many self-appointed experts on The Beatles in Liverpool, some of them qualified and some of them not. I had no obvious credentials to write about them, and one of the things that I was invited to do by Alan Dossor was to go and talk with people who knew them but I said no, I can't do that, I don't research, I am going to write from somewhere more important and he said 'what's that?' and I said 'from the imagination'. Which was probably as pompous as it now sounds. But I had seen a stage documentary about The Beatles that was interesting but it was flat

19

because it had not been fired through the imagination of one author. The theatre is full of historical plays and, after all, that's what The Beatles play was. All right, it was very recent history but, nevertheless, it was an historical play and it struck me then as now that history is baloney, no history can be true. Even if the participants report it, there cannot be one sole truth because, just as if you and I look at that wall and give our impressions of that wall, we are going to give two different impressions. So, 25 people at the Battle of Waterloo are going to tell 25 different stories. So what I did was take the facts and then write my truth about what 'The Beatles' meant. I firmly set myself a task of writing a play about the public face of The Beatles. I was not interested in what John Lennon got up to in bed, what skeletons may or may not be in whatever cupboard because that was not important to me. What was important to me was this amazing phenomenon which had occurred in Liverpool and had touched the lives of so many people. The Beatles' music became a metaphor for so many people, became a reference point for so many people. Now, it seems to me that was worthy of a big play, so I sat down and wrote it in the Everyman house style, gave it to Annie, my wife, to read, by which time I was very dubious about it, and she sat down and read it and she said to me 'it's wonderful'.

I met with Alan Dossor who was to direct the play. He'd read the script and he was extremely agitated. He had some right to be - as delivered the script would have played at about four and a half hours! It was terribly overwritten. At this time Alan taught me a massive amount about the nature of cutting and editing a script. He was quite superb in this. He would say to me, 'Why do you say this on page 34?'and I'd say, 'Well, I like the way in which it is said.' So he'd say, 'Yes. But you've already said it clearly on page 30. The audience has already been given that information.' Inevitably, I suppose, like any young writer I had not learnt to trust the ability of a theatre audience to absorb information and so probably repeated things time and again when it just wasn't necessary. Alan taught me this and taught me how to find the real centre of a scene and to be ruthless about cutting away any dead wood and dross which would ultimately lessen, rather than heighten the scene's ultimate impact. It's probably because of this experience that I've never had any ideological or ego problems when it comes to cutting a script. I would and I do fight fiercely when suggested cuts are simply wrong or damaging but the actual concept of editing and cutting a script is something I've never had a problem with. Indeed, I really enjoy going through the process of improving what is already there. This is probably due to the fact that, unlike some other writers, I've never been the victim of a director taking a script from me, keeping me at some distance and then letting me into a rehearsal to see a scene which had been cut by a hand other than my own. If I had, I would have screamed and, no matter how wise or beneficial the cut, would have insisted on its reinstatement. I would ultimately have been accused of behaving badly. Writers can behave badly but, in my experience, the writer who is behaving badly is usually one who is being treated badly, usually in regard to his text. No matter how overwritten or mis-

20

structured a script, no-one, absolutely no-one but the author has the right to cut or restructure. Many others, directors, actors, audiences, even critics can help him to realise and remedy these problems. But no-one should ever make the mistake of doing it for him. What Alan always did during the early days of The Beatles show was say to me, 'Look, can you come in tonight, I need you to work on the script.' Often he would ask me to look at a particular moment and I would come to understand why I was being asked to re-examine something and then be able to remedy or improve upon it. I benefited enormously from this process and learnt a great deal from it. In the case of that particular play, what came out of this process was a really pared down and clear script. As always seems to be the case, once it had been cut and shaped, the script actually emerged as

Willy Russell and Barbara Dickson at Rockford's in Liverpool in February 1981 to celebrate the Playhouse opening of 'Educating Rita'.

21

a fuller, not a lesser piece of work. I think this period was one in which the playwright/director relationship was at its best. It was not a one way thing, with Alan doing all the giving and me doing all the taking. I think it is fair to say that Alan was probably also learning. Strangely (for a man who had most successfully established a truly popular theatre in Liverpool), he then had no interest in and therefore virtually no knowledge of popular music and its place in society. Because of this, I think that Alan had underestimated the relish with which the audience was going to share this play and it was only really when the play opened that he came to see the full celebratory nature of what we had. There had been many times during the cutting of the script when Alan had asked me to provide more 'explanation' of certain moments and references. This I resisted because, knowing popular music, I knew the audience's foreknowledge of the story we were telling and knew that the audience did not need to have explained what it already knew.

J.G.   Barbara Dickson played the piano, didn't she?

W.R.   Yes, she was staggering. People in the Everyman had never heard that voice before. And not only is Barbara a superb singer, she had the best diction of any popular singer I knew. So I knew she was actually going to place the lyrics superbly. Now it was crucial to me because I had written the play as a musical. I had not just used those songs chronologically, I had used them dramatically, so it was important that we heard the lyrics. So that's why we brought Barbara in. We got to the first preview and it was an extraordinary night in the theatre. When Trevor Eve first walked on in front of Barbara, she was playing 'Your Mother Should Know', he put some money in a tea-vending machine and people in the theatre thought that it was a con within a con, that the play was set up to pretend that The Beatles got together to play under the guise of Wings, and they thought that what we had done was put this play on and this was the real Beatles walking into the Everyman. And then, when Bernard Hill walked on, I mean, looking - I hadn't seen them in costume and make up because I had been teaching all the time, so I was going through the same thing as the audience. The first scene should have played about 4 minutes but eventually lasted about 15 minutes. They couldn't get on with it, the audience were just howling, applauding, laughing - it just went on and on, it was quite extraordinary and it was apparent really from that night that we had something, I mean, quite against expectations.

J.G.   It was at this time that you met another crucial figure, in the form of Peggy Ramsay. Did she approach you or you approach her?

W.R.   Alan Plater said to me when I was adapting 'When the Reds' - 'You should have an agent', and the agent he said I should go to was Peggy Ramsay. And I said 'What's the point?' because we were talking about the biggest drama agent in the world, it would have just been ridiculous, almost pretentious for me to have that sort of agent. I was still a part-time writer. I didn't think she would consider me so I didn't pursue that at all. And then, a few years later, when I was trying to sell a TV play - that one based on the Lucy Wan ballad - I got a letter back from Thames TV or somebody, saying we cannot read plays now unless they are submitted through a literary agent. So I thought, well, if I am going to function in this world, I've got to have a literary agent, so I wrote to Harvey Unna, I'd just picked his name out of a book, he seemed like the second one down from Peggy Ramsay. So I wrote to him and said would you take me on and they wrote back and said we have read your work, it is interesting but we are not interested in taking on writers of films - a letter which they now have framed on their walls. So then, just before rehearsing The Beatles show, I went in for a Radio Times competition which still runs today, I think. You had to write a play, get it sponsored by somebody in the business, and then it would go forward to this competition. I asked Barry Hanson to sponsor my play, it was called 'Death of a Young, Young Man'. He phoned me up on Boxing Day to say that, yes, of course he would sponsor me but more important, that he wanted to buy it. So, I thought, fantastic, I am in with a chance now. A couple of months previously I had been rejected by Yorkshire where there was a fellowship on offer, by a panel including Alan Plater, who had said to me 'look, don't worry, you'll make it anyway' which was no joy to me. There was me teaching, Annie was pregnant, she had stopped teaching and I was desperate to write, desperate; I felt that I was sinking at this time. And so I went for this Radio Times competition, got down there on the day of the interview, met the other three candidates and just as we were sitting there waiting to go in, I said to them 'Well, when's your play going to be transmitted?' Blank looks. None of the other plays had been deemed to be good enough to go into production but mine had. I thought, 'well I must be in with a great chance!' So, I go into the interview, fine ..... come out, sit around while they deliberate. The result was going to be announced before lunch and then we were all going to have lunch at the Radio Times offices. Hugh Whitemore was amongst the judges; they came out and they said, 'you won, Mr So and So, so you get five grand. But Mr So and So and Ms So and So, we thought your work was so good and you are in need of encouragement, so we are going to give each of you £400'. I said 'Now wait a minute.' I was apoplectic with rage. I mean, at least if they'd said to me 'There's 400 quid', which would have meant a fantastic amount at that time, I wouldn't have felt so totally rejected. What I couldn't get my head round was - I'd written a play that was going out on 'Play for Today' in six months time. Surely, I was a dramatist, worth encouraging. I was so angry. There was a huge cabinet with booze in it, I thought 'I'm not staying with this', so I grabbed hold of a bottle of scotch and left. Hugh Whitemore followed me out, and said 'Don't go, Don't go'. He said 'Listen, I completely understand your anger and what a travesty and all that, but just forget it.' I beat it down the stairs. Hugh was trying to calm me down, and he said to me 'Look, this is stupid: I really want to do something, at least give me your permission to take this script to Peggy Ramsay'. I said 'You can

23

take it to who the hell you want' and I left. I can't remember coming home. I must have been steaming. I got into school the next day and I was teaching with a terrible hangover when somebody came in and said 'There's a woman on the phone for you, I told her you are teaching and she said ''Close the school down and get him out. I'm not having teaching interfering with important things, dear''.' I walked into the staff room and on the phone was Peggy. 'Why dear, what are you doing, dear? You're standing up in front of boys and girls are you? How charming! Tom, he really is teaching! Now listen, darling, I am going to represent you,' she said 'Do you want any dough?' All I knew was, somebody in her position had tracked me down to Shorefields School. I knew that she was serious, that this woman didn't mess about. She was far too big and busy. So the sub-text of the conversation was, here was a real judge of drama, who thought it was important enough to track me down at the school. God knows how she found out where I was and to this day I don't know.

J.G.   Didn't Hugh Whitemore have anything to do with that?

W.R.   No, Hugh didn't know where I worked in terms of school and all that, but Hugh had taken the script round and said - read this. He was one of her writers in those days. Anyway, Peggy said 'When you go home tonight, get everything you've written, put it into an envelope and just send it to me. Every single thing'. So I went home and got together this huge bundle of stuff and I sent it down.

She telephoned one evening about quarter to seven and she's a very voluble person, you know. Once she's off on a kick it's very difficult to get a word in edgeways. Anyway, she'd just read 'John, Paul, George, Ringo ... and Bert' and she just thought it sensational, and I kept trying to get a word in edgeways and the next thing is there's a taxi at the door and she just doesn't want to listen while she talks, she doesn't know the meaning of the word pause. So you can't leap in anywhere and, at the end of this 50 minute session she said 'and we've got to do something about getting this play on, dear'. I said 'Peggy, I'm awfully sorry to be rude but the taxi's waiting at the door because I'm going to the first night now'. She said 'What? You've got it on? Tom - he's brilliant, he's got it on all on his own'. So it was very, very important to me that I had Peggy, because what happened then was, it went from a little play designed for three weeks, into something that was extremely hot, and within two days of the reviews coming out, we had wall-to-wall producers in the Everyman, from the West End. There are still unscrupulous people in the business and I remember a moment when I was standing at the bar at 6 o clock, and two very unlikely characters to be in The Bistro in those days, dressed in very expensive suits sidled up to me and said 'Are you Willy Russell?' I said 'Yes' and they said 'Well, where can we be alone - we've flown in to acquire the rights to your play. We have with us at the moment £1,000 in cash which we'd like to give you for an option on the play.' Fortunately, I had Peggy to deal with all that sort of stuff. If it had happened to me when I was 18 years of age, I might have been tempted

Willy Russell at work!

but I suppose having been brought up to always be suspicious of easy money, something said no this isn't right. I called Alan Dossor and he took them out and saw them off. I think even then I knew that's not the way that producers should behave. The producer who struck me as the only one I wanted to do business with really was Michael Codron. Michael was charm itself, but Peggy didn't want Michael to produce the play alone as he'd never done a musical. Bob Swash came up; Bob Swash was then the head of the theatre division of the Robert Stigwood group and was such a nice man, he didn't seem like one's idea of a producer. We stood at the bar for about an hour afterwards and he talked about all sorts of things, apart from theatre and the play. Then Stigwood himself came over from L.A. He came the night that Peggy came with David Hare. David Hare was terrified because he was then writing 'Teeth 'n' Smiles', a play about a rock band at Cambridge and he heard from Peggy about this play of mine and thought that he was writing a play which had just been written, so he had to come and check it out and make sure that his play wasn't a double, which of course it's not - completely different piece of work. So Stigwood was up that night, Peggy, David Hare, a lot of other people, who I didn't recognise then, and that day Annie went into hospital to have Robert. I came from the hospital at about 9 o'clock into the theatre, and I was watching from the back

25

with another mate of mine who I'd not really spoken to for a while, because we'd had a very bad holiday together. But he'd just recently had a child and he brought a bottle of champagne down to the theatre, so by half past 10 when the play ended, I was gaga and I remember marching through a door and knocking this woman over. Alan Dossor came and said 'Peggy Ramsay - meet Willy Russell'. She taught me a hell of a lot about how to behave because these were very heady times. If I'd had that sort of over-night success as an 18 or 19 year old, I might well have been a rock and roll victim. But when all the madness started, I had Peggy to look to. She had a great sense of proportion in all things and she always urged me, 'Behave well, darling - behave well'.

J.G.   Is that one of the reasons why you stayed in Liverpool, to feel comfortable and you learned if you went and lived in London you'd be lionised in every wine bar in Hampstead?

W.R.   Some chance! Many writers in London write for the theatre goers, they write as though they are at the centre of the debate and the fact that their plays may only be produced once at one of the large, susidised theatres doesn't seem to impinge upon them as being significant. No, to me it matters. If I wrote a play no matter how widely it was reviewed and praised, if it did not play in other towns, other cities, other countries, I would think there was something wrong with the play.

J.G.   It seems to me you are operating with a delicate balance between very high standards of professionalism and, at the same time, addressing a market that hasn't traditionally been theatre-goers.

W.R.   But never, I hope, at the expense of the theatre-goer. I hope I don't address this wide audience at the expense of the more informed audience.

J.G.   Could we pick up the theme of education? There are several educationalists in the plays: Frank in 'Rita', Kidder in 'One Summer', Mrs Kay in 'Our Day Out'.

W.R.   Costas in 'Shirley Valentine'.

J.G.   An educationalist?

W.R.   Yes, in his own way. He's not dissimilar from those other characters.

J.G.   You mean not in a formal sense, fashioned in a classroom, but in the sense of educating a woman about life? You'd seriously place him in that group?

W.R.   Yes, she says 'He didn't say anything. He sat down and stared at the sea with me and he knew when it was all right to speak.' That's a man who knows, he gave her time and space. I'm not making inflated claims for Costas. What I am

26

saying is that if you wanted to look at it in that light, you could see that again dramatically it's using a force from, as it were another culture in order to lay stepping stones for another human being. And that role is one that is often present in my plays. Epstein in The Beatles play can be seen as that conduit.

J.G.   Is it the A.S.Neill tradition of educating, and would you say that you are definitely against the more authoritarian style of teaching?

W.R.   Totally. It is not the way to convert human beings; to suppress in the human being is to deny it. You've got to acknowledge all the elements of humanity, not try and suppress them, including the base and the vile and potentially the evil. Now it seems to me that people like Neill would acknowledge these things in humanity but he wouldn't, therefore, try to suppress people. I'm not saying that he has all the answers to the world's problems, he doesn't, but I think he is on a more sure path than the likes of Norman Tebbitt.

J.G.   Fair enough. Well, what is your philosophy of life? I know that sounds a pretentious question, but is there an underlying philosophy that informs everything you do?

W.R.   I don't think I've got a thoroughly articulated philosophy. Something you've probably heard me say is that I always reserve the right to cancel on Wednesday everything I said on Tuesday. But I think that in a sense is part of the philosophy, the philosophy of not being completely definite.

J.G.   So you are pragmatic?

W.R.   It's certainly pragmatic. As a teacher I would sometimes be extremely authoritarian when it was required but I was never hijacked by that role. With my own kids I would sometimes be completely liberal, other times I would be authoritarian. Somebody once said of somebody, 'He had that rarest of qualities, common sense.' It is a very rare quality common sense, and that's all I try; to go through life and deal with it in those terms and using, to be specific, common sense because it does have in it the suggestion of the community. It is common to all, it is what would benefit all. I don't have any 'isms'; I am not an idealogue. I am much more pragmatic. There have been times where ideologies have been central to the salvation of a people. And times where an ideology has been the cause of unpardonable suffering.

J.G.   Can you be more specific? I'm trying to get your philosophy of life in a nutshell.

W.R.   Well, I don't think you will because I would shy away from that. I always do and I'm not interested in having anything to encompass me in that way.

J.G.   What about a definition like 'a humanitarian tinged with socialist ideas'?

Willy Russell at his old college (now called South Mersey College, Childwall) in October 1986.

Willy Russell at the Central Library, Liverpool in March 1982 to open an exhibition of the work of the Open University.

Willy Russell at Liverpool University, July 1990, receiving an Honorary Doctorate. (Gordon Whiting)

W.R. Well I always use these phrases, humanitarian and humanist, but to be quite honest if you pin me down and said to me 'define it' I would be at a loss. But I use it as a means of indicating the broad area of operation.

J.G. So the central targets of 'Blood Brothers' wouldn't be politically direct, it's more to do with a sense of injustice or imbalance in society that people were suffering simply by being born into them?

W.R. The conditions that the characters in 'Blood Brothers' lived through are conditions that were brought about just as much by Labour as by the Conservative government, if you think about it. The whole life-span of the Johnstones covers more Labour years. With 'Breezeblock Park', I think people thought this was a deeply political play. It was written during the term of a Labour government. It seemed to me when I was writing back in the 70s, and it would be the same today, that we had a situation where there was a great worshipping at the shrine of the Welfare State and the feeling was, well how can these people complain; they've got houses, they've got schools; for those of them who can't function in the labour market they've got the DHSS. I mean, nobody ever seemed to address themselves to the fact that spiritually these people were caving in. That the Welfare State, as crucial, as venerable, as necessary as many of its institutions were, needed a re-examination. The thin end of it had come about to meet very specific needs at a very specific time, but by the time you got to the early 70s, I mean, the Welfare State was actually helping many of the ills to fester. There was no doubt about it, when I watched TV it was usually poor women from Kirkby talking about 'like what we haven't got from the Social...' an inbred Welfare State mentality, 'The government are not looking after me' was a common cry. 'They've not done this for us' and 'They've not done that for us', but nobody used to bat an eyelid. Now, because of Labour's failure to address itself to that, it was very easy for the Conservatives to walk in and tackle the situation. It needed addressing a long time before that. We needed to say: 'It's not enough to be put out at Kirkby, with all the grants and the fact that you can live on the dole.' People were going nuts. Just go and look at doctors' prescriptions for Valium, that should tell you the state of the spiritual health of the nation. What were the unions doing during those years? More money, more money, more money. Did they ever cut overtime? I can't remember any union leader who tried to abolish overtime for its members.

J.G. So would you say that you are not a slave to any political party?

W.R. No, no. I mean, look, I am instinctively left. I'm always on the side of people who - let me get this right because I don't want to be sentimental - I'm always on the side of people who are trying to work it out in some way.

J.G. And do your ideas cut across mere party lines? Is it much more important than that, but you have an allegiance to more disadvantaged people?

W.R. I don't have a rose-tinted view of the working class. I never have had. And I've always had an objectivity about the working class that enables me to write about it. But really I don't write about the working class, I write about characters who come from it. There are elements of some of it which are so bigoted, so conservative, so tribal. Some of it is appalling; I mean some of the radio I listen to, I want to stop the car and shoot myself sometimes, it's pandering to the lowest common denominator. My attitude is akin to the old BBC idea, to entertain and educate. It's very unfashionable to say those things now, but I do believe in them. I do believe that one shouldn't ever cave in to the lowest common denominator, because it is not really there. Most taste is dictated out of commercial and political quarters, anyway.

J.G. You are whole-hearted in supporting educational projects, aren't you? There isn't a politician in your work is there, but there are creative, educational people.

W.R. I think there is some sort of quiet, crusading philosophy and voice at work there, yes. It's allied with certain movements that I could point to, but again I would probably not join a specific movement. You could say that I have a lot of sympathy with the humanist movement, I have a lot of sympathy with the Quaker movement, I have a lot of sympathy with the hippie movement; but in each of those three, just to select three examples at random, some of it is appalling, and that's why I cannot embrace a totalised ideology.

J.G. In the last analysis, is it Willy Russell, a powerful, great individualist who takes from various streams of thought whatever he thinks is the most effective?

W.R. It's not great and powerful, it's fiercely individual. We must have two things really - and this sounds terribly wishy-washy - we must have a society in which there really is equal opportunity for all, which is what the 1944 Act was about; equal opportunity, not equality, which it was often mistaken for in the 60s, but we must have a society which allows for all individuals. The problem is, I find it very difficult to talk about these things in abstract terms because they are not abstractions, they are practical matters and so when I make a statement like that, I am talking about somebody living in England at the end of the 20th century. I couldn't make that statement if I was living in the Third World today, because one would have to make such fundamental decisions that, for example, you might for a period of time have to trample the voice of the individual - or you might say no, we'll go with the individual and then we'd see millions go to the wall. But, as I say, I can't talk about these things in abstract terms because it depends what we are talking about, when and in what particular place. And that's why, to go back, I'd be pragmatic rather than ideological.

31

J.G.   Yes, quite. Let's be pragmatic about 'Breezeblock Park', then. Who are the characters in 'Breezeblock Park' based on? Can you name names on that?

W.R.   Yes, yes. Very much my Auntie Dolly.

J.G.   Is she the person Betty was based on?

W.R.   Yes, but only as a starting point, she became an amalgam, there's some of my mother in there. There's a lot of my mother in Sandra, my mother when she was younger. There's some of my dad in Ted. My Uncle Dick was definitely Syd, my Uncle Stan is Tommy.

J.G.   And what was their reaction when they saw the play?

W.R.   They never saw it. For years I didn't let out any hint of the fact that they were involved in it, but then Dolly got to know. It's slightly convoluted; my secretary's sister had just gone in to hospital for an exploratory breast lump, fortunately it proved to be nothing. Now Rozzie, who had seen this play was on the same ward as my Auntie Dolly. My Auntie Dolly was saying such things as 'My nephew is Willy Russell'. So Rozzie said 'Oh I know Willy', and halfway through this conversation Rozzie said 'Oh you're the woman from ''Breezeblock Park'' '. Of course Dolly was made up that she'd been put into a play. The fact that whoever it was was pilloried was irrelevant. The fact is she'd been immortalised in a play. But, it would be false of me to take these people to the theatre and say, 'Come and see this play that I've written about you' because it is not the case, I go back to what I said, I am not a documentarist. I did think back to a few things that happened and the whole impression of the play is a fairly accurate impression of our family. I have to say it is very like conversations that would happen in our house. I mean, off the wall, and massively theatrical. They'd never had anything to do with the theatre but the whole style in our house was terribly histrionic. It's like in 'Shirley Valentine' when she says of Gillian, I could say it absolutely about Dolly and Edna. If you've got a headache, they've got a brain tumour. Everything was just amplified out of all proportions. I identify so closely when I watch Woody Allen pictures, because Woody always slips in the Jewish family scene. It is very like working class Liverpudlians, I feel so at home with that. When I walked into our house the first thing I got was a lowdown on who's dead from the <u>Echo</u>, who's suffering from what, in whispered tones, who's doing what with whom. But I love that stuff you see.

J.G.   And does this apply to all the characters in all the plays, that there's a great deal of people you know in each of them?

W.R.   No, I couldn't tell you where the models came from in 'Blood Brothers'. I haven't a clue where any of those came from.

J.G.   Was Mrs Stubbs in 'Lies' a prototype of Mrs Johnstone?

W.R.   Yes, I was working out that thing about her dancing. You'll also see, I think, that she's probably even more in the mother in 'Death of a Young, Young Man'.

J.G.   Really? Is the spud picking in 'Death of a Young, Young Man' based on your own experience?

W.R.   Absolutely. We went spud picking and we used to cycle from Knowsley down the East Lancs Road to Blindfoot Lane. There's an old Roman coach road, it's just sensational, between Bickerstaffe and Rainford. Up there are a lot of big farms which were not oversubscribed. We knew that, because we went to school in Rainford. Most of the picking around Knowsley was oversubscribed and it wasn't worth doing the job.

J.G.   So is Billy you?

W.R.   To a certain extent, yes.

J.G.   His mates Bo and Cazza, are they your pals?

W.R.   No, because I used to really distance myself from them. I would always do that. Kids would go over the top, I would try and persuade them out of it, I would not be as daft as that. When I was about 13/14, I did go and pick for a week on a farm down there. Now normally you only ever last a day then you're moved on. But I got down to this farm and this fellow offered us something like one pound a day. It was a fantastic piece of luck and it was a very easy field to pick. Some are bitches because of prickles. Topping we were doing and I remember a day, it was very early October, a really beautiful, warm autumn day, just picking this field by myself, I mean it was like being on a different planet. It did make a big impression on me, being taken on at that farm. I don't know why. Unlike most farmers who are pretty bluff and very heavy towards Liverpudlians out that way, this guy was sort of a Kidder figure and a Mrs Kaye figure. He wasn't afraid of kids and people with Liverpool accents. And he didn't come on with the big macho.

J.G.   Wilson was his name in the play?

W.R.   Wilson, that's right, yes.

J.G.   What about the Benny figure, the one who's a bit simple and shoots Billy at the end? Is he an invention of yours?

W.R. I was brought up at a time when you still did have idiots in the community. 'Slow people', 'backward people', 'remedial people', 'dimwits'. It was common that. They were part of the community, so one was aware of them and yet I suspect that character is cribbed from literature rather than life. To be quite honest it smacks of John Steinbeck really.

J.G. Are certain plays more a job of work as distinct from plays fired by your real enthusiasm and imagination? Does that mean that you treat them in a more perfunctory way, just like a job?

W.R. Yes, you have to flog yourself. You see, in those days you could do it, you could do jobs of work for TV, because there were the slots available. It was rather like radio is today, there's lots of jobbing writing goes on in radio. We don't have it in TV drama now.

J.G. Is 'Break In' like that?

W.R. Certainly - 'Break In' and 'Lies'.

J.G. What other plays fall into this category?

W.R. 'I Read the News Today', the radio play. I suppose 'The Boy with the Transistor Radio' although I felt it was transformed in the making into something better, I was trying to do something big with it as well, but we couldn't do all that fantasy stuff. But yes, when I say jobbing I don't mean one is being cynical about it. It is not a question of that, but in those days it was a question of being tied into one of those commissions, I'd have to do it. Don't forget, 'Break In' was commissioned after The Beatles show opened at the Everyman but certainly before it had gone into the West End or anything like that and I needed to earn money.

J.G. In 'Break In', is Macka, the central character, based on anyone?

W.R. No, what interested me more in 'Break In', and I still think it's an interesting idea as a play, was I wanted to write about a group of kids who go into a school and then the following day the adults walk in and it looks like they've smeared paint everywhere. But what we see is there was no malevolence on their part, they weren't trying to hurt anybody else, they were creating, let loose in this school, with all things at their disposal. And it's framed in a bit of a plot. You know, one had to write a strong plot for kids.

J.G. So when you were at school you had a clear idea of your ability in English, but you felt that it couldn't come out because the teachers were so unsympathetic?

W.R. To an 11 year old boy from a rural village in Knowsley to end up in Woolfall Secondary School, was traumatic. There's no doubt about it, but the problem for me was, I was never seen as one of the traumatised, sensitive souls. My parents always used to say to me, the problem with you is because you're big, people don't know that you are sensitive. They always said that to me, you know. Now I didn't quite understand what they were saying, but I knew that they recognised something in me that was important to me. I was this thing that they called 'sensitive'. I wasn't somebody who wanted to be out there sticking the nut on people and all that. Yet I could look after myself in that area as well, you see. So I didn't personally get a lot of physical abuse from the thugs in the playground, because I looked like I could hold my own corner, but I used to see less fortunate kids than me. You know what they are like in the playground, they sniff and they smell the weak and they go for them and they cripple them. They cripple the cripples. You see what real animals human beings are when you go to an institution like that. I was not often personally bullied but I loathed the brutality that surrounded me. The staff was running in fear, it was a chaotic, badly run school. The staff were probably sitting there thinking what the hell they were doing teaching in a dive like this. The headmaster was just a monster. I was just so relieved to get out of that school after the first year, and what suited me down to the ground about the school at Rainford was that after this urban nightmare, I was back in the tranquility of the country. Even though the school was really Edwardian in attitude, it suited me because I knew what the rules were. At Woolfall you didn't know what the rules were.

J.G. Could most of your work be seen as being autobiographical?

W.R. I suppose, inevitably, it is autobiographical, but autobiography is never my aim and it is never a conscious starting point. I am not a writer who ever researches and if I had to research then I would never write. I feel that if I have to research, then I don't know it within me. I sometimes find when writing a play that I will (rather than stopping the writing in order to conduct some research), loot my own past in order to inform certain aspects of the character, which is why Rita is a ladies' hairdresser. Because I have done that job, I could have her speak with authority. In 'Blood Brothers' there is a moment in Act Two when a teacher asks a question. I remember I was borrowing from my time as a teacher. But on a probably far more important level it seems to me looking back at the plays that they are not autobiographical. I am not consciously exploring myself. I am certainly not trying to work something out. The fact that I went through a struggle to get back into education is not for example something I am trying to resolve in my work. I am not angst-ridden about that, I dealt with it in life.

J.G. So is it too glib and simplistic to see your whole work in terms of having a single theme running through it, to do with an individual from the working class breaking away from imprisoning family and social circumstances?

W.R.   Sounds glib to me, when it is put like that. Because what that does is to deny all sorts of other things which I hope are present in my work, or swamps other things that are in my work. Yes, it is true of 'Educating Rita', which is absolutely about breaking free of something that is quintessentially working class, but the play is also intended to appeal to people who have got no experience whatsoever of working class life. So that definition might be a springboard but it is not the be all and end all.

J.G.   You say the way you regard the creative process is that the author doesn't pick his theme, rather the theme is a product of the author himself, of his life and experiences, and so it is almost pre-determined by the life that you have lived. So, how does the play evolve? You mentioned before to me that you hear a voice inside you; now I remember you said you couldn't explain what this voice was, but interpreting it as your creative imagination, do you find an authentic voice within you and it develops out of that?

W.R.   I was sitting in the garden the other day and I found myself thinking about the beginnings of a play, in film terms actually, and I could see a central character but I couldn't hear it. I work my life in voices, I am working in different voices and accents all the time. So it is often as basic as that, of me being able to bring it out of my imagination and turn it into something real and tangible that I can crack a gag with, entertain with - and if I can entertain a couple of people in here for two minutes with a voice, the chances are it might be an interesting voice to look at on the stage. Because that's what characters are on stage, I am using the word 'voice' but you could even use the word character because if you get a voice right, from inside, it suggests an entire character. I don't mean just aping an accent. For instance, I was listening to Rod Steiger giving an interview last night and he was talking about his work on accents and it was the same thing; getting the Jewish accent right in 'The Pawnbroker' was the whole key to the performance of that role. Even though he was speaking about acting, rather then writing, I knew exactly what he meant. For my part, getting the voice of Rita or the voice of Shirley Valentine right was, in each case, the key into the whole play.

J.G.   I think your work has a great deal of unity; there is always a tone of humanity, with an empathy for the characters, as well as a critical detachment from them. In terms of language, there is the authentic Liverpool dialect that you use and then this idea about individuals escaping from certain problematical situations in family and society, moving towards a greater sense of personal choice and freedom. There seems to be a unity in the plays as a whole, along those lines. Is that a fair assessment?

W.R.   Yes. It is inevitable, isn't it? If you look at the work of anybody, of any writer you will find this unless he is perversely eclectic. You look at Ayckbourn today, who is trying, almost self-consciously, to work in different forms. The other day John Peter compared a play written in 1972 with a play written in 1990, and found them to be vastly different in style, but absolutely common to the man, to the writer; and I suppose it is true of me. You could lump together the plays that you have just described, the music I have written, the songs that I have written, the bits of acting I have done, the bits of directing I have done, and you'll probably see one thing shot through all of them because the one thing that is common to them is this guy talking.

J.G.   That wouldn't be the case with Alan Bleasdale, would it, because his work traverses a wider field of subject matter, surely? For example Percy Toplis, in 'The Monocled Mutineer', Elvis Presley in 'Are You Lonesome Tonight?', Yosser in 'Boys from the Blackstuff', and then The Irish Question in 'No Surrender'. Surely there is a greater ranging around a wider field of themes in his work; or is that a false notion?

Willy Russell and Alan Bleasdale at the Everyman Theatre in March 1992 to unveil a plaque marking a 10-year sponsorship from Whitbread.

W.R.   I think it is a false notion. It is not a question of themes but a question of settings. The same themes crop up in Alan's work; what he has done is relocate it in a 1920's war situation, or in an Orange and Green situation, so he might, because of that, touch upon issues which I don't. For example, I would run a mile from dealing with topical issues, I don't begin plays from the point of view of 'issues', because I think I write more from a philosophical/political perspective, than a social/political perspective. So I think it is completely possible to work within one square mile and write about the whole of humanity, the whole universe. Go back to Jane Austen, who never left one village in her life, and touched on the scale of human relationships from A to Z. Other, more widely travelled writers, whose work might reflect the fact of that travel, can try to touch on wider issues, but fail miserably when compared with her.

J.G.   Let's try to get to the bottom of what you said about the philosophical/political perspective that you use. Can you try to define it?

W.R.   I think it goes back to the fact that I don't start from issues. I don't isolate issues and say 'I am now going to write about that' because I try not to write problem plays. There is a problem in society that an author addresses, and in the theatre it is called the problem play. At its most obvious, we need a pedestrian crossing in Woolton, we haven't got one, so a writer in the community sits down and writes a half hour play for the local community about that. Now the function of that play is to get a crossing, and like the function of a play to get rid of a Thatcher government, it is a 'problem play'. I am not putting any sort of value judgement on this, but I am not interested in writing this sort of play, something which deals with a specific problem and because of that tends to have no sub-text and no philosophical underbelly. Better to my mind, is the play which has a sub-text, which has a philosophical underbelly and which might still deal with a contemporary problem. The play that I would want to write would have something at the centre of it which was recognizable to a contemporary audience, and would be as recognizable to an audience 500 years previous and 500 years hence, and in Botswana as well as Prescot. And I am sure that Alan would say exactly the same thing. This is why 'Educating Rita' is not a problem play, it is not the problem of that girl persuading the authorities to give her a grant. It is the problem of every human being who wanted something that was being denied them, and who then found herself trying to make life better for herself, which means that the play has what I call this philosophical under-belly. This is the sort of play that interests me, and it is what I want to write but I go back to what we said before; you can write that in a square mile. Woody Allen does it all the time. And I see Woody Allen primarily as a writer (or value him more as a writer than as a director). You know, he just won't move out of New York, you see the same locations, the same delis, the same diners..., but he is telling huge human stories, which could have been told 500 years ago or 500 years hence - of course the setting would be different. If you are dealing

Willy Russell and Barbara Dickson in Liverpool, December 1982.

with what goes on in the minds and hearts of human beings, then you are aiming to explore and to whittle down something which is primarily philosophical rather than social. It will have a social function but it goes beyond that and above that.

J.G.   So any political implications are, in effect, very secondary? I mean in the case of 'Blood Brothers', does it deliberately engage with the social problems of the 80's?

W.R.   That intention has often been claimed for the play on my behalf by enthusiastic commentators; now I don't stand up and deny that my perception of prevailing social conditions are woven into the fabric of the play; but I didn't say I am writing 'Blood Brothers' in order to highlight these appalling conditions in the later half of the 20th century. I was primarily interested in the fundamental issues of what was happening between these human beings, a woman, who did a deal to swap a baby.

J.G.   You were thinking of writing 'Blood Brothers' for your R.S.C. Commission, and you were put off by some pretentious person, weren't you?

W.R.   It was the one I had in my back pocket. Walter Donohue, the then literary manager of the R.S.C., who I have a lot of respect for, wanted to commission me and he asked me to go to London to meet a director called Bill Alexander. I met him in a pub, and it seemed to me patently obvious that Bill Alexander didn't have a clue who I was and he thought Walter was a bit of a pain in the neck for bringing all these young writers into the Warehouse. So he gave me rather a perfunctory glance and I found myself spieling 'Blood Brothers'. I obviously was not well prepared for this meeting, I was two lines in and he said 'Oh yes, I see, a sort of socio-economic blah blah' - I said to Walter, I'm going now, and I left him in the pub.

J.G.   Let's talk about the first night of 'Blood Brothers' at the Liverpool Playhouse in January '83.

W.R.   The terror of creating a play in the first place is so huge, that it is far easier to cope with the terror of a first night. We'd had real terror during the first preview of 'Blood Brothers' because we found that the sound quality in the theatre wasn't what we thought it was going to be and the person who was responsible for it at the Playhouse had just not handled it well. At that first preview, during the interval Bob Swash, the producer, Chris Bond, the director, myself and Pete Filleul who was then the musical orchestrator, met in the bar and we were all suicidal because we felt that the audience just thought it was complete and utter rubbish. That's when we said about bringing in the right sound guys and we went back in to what we thought was a really desultory second half and we were prepared to go working into the night. But this audience went absolutely ecstatic, so you can get an audience really badly wrong before you get them right from standing at the back. That might have been our collective nerves of course, or maybe it was the fact that it was the first preview and people were a bit nervous as to what to expect. In New York you never trust your preview audience because they are always ecstatic and here was a preview audience that seemed like it was in church being numbed by a sermon. But I remember the first night as the curtain came down, I stood at the back with tears just flowing down quietly from my face, not out of joy but out of sheer relief. It had been such a long, hard job and to know that we'd got there was just absolute relief, you know, there wasn't a feeling of 'Wow, we've made it and it's brilliant'. There was just - emptiness, really, we were washed out. Anyway, that was the first night of 'Blood Brothers'. I can't remember the performance, I can't remember anything in particular, because you've got to the first night, there is nothing more you can do, and I usually nip out for a smoke or a drink, then nip back in, because it really is solely in the hands of the actors.

J.G.   Is the first night in America more daunting than a first night in Liverpool?

W.R.   No, Liverpool is the most daunting of all, right, but I'll get back to that in a minute. What is daunting in America is the fact that the future of the play in question is going to be determined by the opinion of one man in the New York Times. So you've got that really rather unreal situation to contend with in America. No, for me, Liverpool is the worst, principally because I live and work here and if I stand in a theatre on 42nd Street and a play of mine doesn't work there, well I'm going to be on a plane and home within a few days. I can in a sense leave it behind me. The same is true of London. Here, if I get something wrong, I meet people who were there, and you know what they're like here. They are not slow in telling you that you've got it wrong and often it can be something that's not much to do with you, but they'll think here because you wrote it, you are responsible for the whole shamoodle. So, Liverpool means more to me on a first night than anywhere, I suppose.

J.G.   Are you wounded by criticism?

W.R.   Oh, yes. Especially unfair criticism.

J.G.   Do you find Liverpool people more critical of your work?

W.R.   No, I haven't had a lot of adverse criticism, I'm happy to say, because there's no bullshit, it is one of those no bullshit languages. Whereas somebody in a different part of the world might, you know, respectfully suggest that perhaps ... and the whole business is convoluted; I prefer the Liverpool criticism 'You fucked that up didn't you?' And especially if somebody comes out and puts themselves on the line. I hate that sort of weevilling criticism where somebody doesn't want to come out and put themselves on the line and say 'I think you've

41

got it wrong here'. You can cope with that, you can enter into a debate then. Put it on the nose and I can deal with it. Newspaper criticism I never deal with, I've never, ever responded to a newspaper or journal criticism, and sometimes I've been very tempted to. John Peter wrote a review of 'Educating Rita' that made the play transfer from a tiny studio theatre into the West End. There is no doubt that that review had a great influence on the future of that play and one feels 'Oh I must write to him', but why? He is a critic doing his job, I'm a playwright, I've done my job, so I don't and equally, I never write when they're pillorying me. I don't get involved in any way with critics, because as I say, they've got their job to do, I've got my job to do. What does offend me greatly is when a critic gets it badly wrong. Mark Stein, for example, in his attack on 'Blood Brothers' in this latest production, impugned me for being an inept lyricist. And as part of his essay, in order to demonstrate the fact, he quoted examples of my lyrics and misquoted them. So he was indicting me for lyrics that I hadn't written, publishing them as if I had written them. Now that seems to me to be power cut loose, inexcusable. But still, I didn't write to the guy.

J.G.   So, is the truth very important to you? Generally speaking, is it a vital part of your approach to people and life?

W.R.   I think the truth is a very potent force and it must be handled with care. I'm not one of those people who say 'I'll bluffly tell the bloody truth, damn the consequences'. The truth often has to be used sparingly. The truth of behaviour is something that is crucial to me. Because when you have untruths, when you have what happened in 'Blood Brothers' for example, then you can cause a volcano to erupt. It is very interesting just reading 'A Doll's House' which I avoided for years because when I was at college the play had been produced in a production by Trevor Nunn, and it was hailed as the original feminist play. I wasn't interested in reading a problem play, so I avoided that and then years later I did read it in a translation by Christopher Hampton and I realised, of course, it's not a mere problem play. It might deal with feminist issues, but the whole springboard of the play is a lie, it's guilt. She lies to her husband about money and that's what starts the cracks. I am just at the moment reading 'Hedda Gabler' and there's deceit. She has led Tesman to believe that she can have a happy marriage with him and she can't. And she has concealed that from Tesman but allowed people like Brack in on the facts. Now that sort of untruth is something that I would not want to live my life by but I can quite understand why some people, like Mrs Johnstone, like Hedda Gabler, like Nora, are actually driven to do that.

J.G.   Can you define what you do as a writer?

W.R.   As I say in 'Not Quite an Introduction', anybody else has just as valid a view of what I'm up to as I do. I don't have the definitive statement because part of the very process of writing is itself instinctive and mysterious. I don't want to shroud it in mystery and mystique but there is no escaping the fact that there is a crucial element which will always be elusive. Why is it that some days things just go well - and they really do - and other days, I mean, I have been working for the last five days on literally three verses of three different songs. It can get like that. Largely because I'm trying to get the structure of it right. But I can't just sit down and work on the structure, I have to wait until there's a bit of flying imagination to the structure that can then be applied to it.

J.G.   Do you really know if you have got an idea that works, because it registers clearly and strongly?

W.R.   That is a lot of what being a writer is about. It is being able to smell it and I use smell as a metaphorical way of saying recognise it because recognise is not as potent a word, it is not potent enough to describe the process. Smell is nearer but I don't want to be mystical about it or idiosyncratic, that is what the process of writing is, it is actually finding something so diamond simple that it will constantly shine through when you are trying to talk about the huge universal things, you will be anchored, you will have that beacon to always go for. Samuel Goldwyn always used to say to his writers 'come in, you've got one minute to tell me the story of the picture you want to sell to me'. One minute. I mean, it sounds very sort of fixed market that, but it's perfect, because all the great stories you can reduce to tell in one minute, and in doing so will suggest the whole macro aspect of the story. Whereas, somebody who came and said 'well, the thing is Sam ...' They couldn't pin the story down, the chances are there wouldn't be a story there.

J.G.   How particular are you about professional standards in the theatre?

W.R   Totally. I remember from when I used to perform myself. You turn up to play a gig and you are supposed to start at 8. The audience has turned up to see you at 8. But nothing starts happening till 20 minutes to 9. The dynamics of the evening are out of the window. A good performance can turn it round but you have to work twice as hard just to undo that failure to organise. You go to the theatre and it's 2 minutes past 8 and the curtain's not come up. I don't mind if somebody walks in front of the curtain and says 'Ladies and gentlemen, we have a problem back-stage because Miss Tendril has found her yellow tights are brown but we will start in 5 minutes time'. Fine, I can cope with that because then it'll just be that 5 minutes. It's things, as basic as that, that have a great effect on theatre. I can remember in the old days when I used to whinge on about it - I still do really - but the theatrical experience for the audience begins hours before they even get to the theatre, often it begins months before when they buy the tickets, their first contact with the theatre. As a playwright, I have always tried to be involved with all that side of things, I don't mean dictating terms, dominating or anything like that. I remember with 'Blood Brothers' at the

43

Playhouse, the publicity people asked what can we tell them about 'Blood Brothers'? 'Look, the easiest thing to tell them is - what were the audience figures for "One for the Road" "Educating Rita" "Stags and Hens" and "Breezeblock Park" at the Playhouse Theatre?' They said 'Sold out'. I said 'Fine, print "One for the Road" was sold out straight away'. You try and control what happens in a box office. I remember when we were doing 'Educating Rita' at the Playhouse, they didn't know they had this monster on their hands and these women in the box office had been used to 30% capacity but four days after 'Educating Rita' opened these women were going nuts. I said to the director 'What are we doing about the the box office staff?' 'What do you mean?' As if they weren't part of the theatre. I went out to a florist and I bought two big bunches of flowers, walked in and said to the people in the box office 'Listen, I know you're working really hard doing this and I would just like to say thanks'. It makes a huge difference and again I don't mean to be patronising. At least I had recognised the fact, I can't take away all the ringing phones but I know that your element of this enterprise needs to be taken into account. And often you get that in the theatre, we all sit and worship at the shrine of the dilemma of what's happening on the stage and forget other things.

J.G. Do you remember your Edinburgh Festival triple bill? The group from St Katherine's was called Cateysaints, only you spelt it with a 'C' rather than a 'K' so it would be higher up in the list.

W.R. Absolutely.

J.G. So people looking down the list would pick you up first.

W.R. That's show business, you know, both words. There is often a confusion and people think of theatre as being somehow rather effete and literary and it's not. It's a sprawling old circus, an old tent, a market place, a flea-pit, that sort of theatre at its best is triumphantly bawdy, abrasive and often sensitive, subtle, telling - all those things are possible. There seems to be this sort of dichotomy in English culture that you can't be Rabelaisian and fine both at the same time.

J.G. What is 'Educating Rita' about?

W.R. What the film and the play are about is not really somebody who has to be educated but about somebody who had to arrive at a point in her life where she had more control over her life, more choice. She says 'I don't know how I'll exercise that choice, I might have a baby. I might go back to me mother's, I might go to Australia'. Her actual choice is not important, what decision she comes up with is not important. She tells Frank 'what's important is you have brought me to this stage in my life where I can have the exercise of choice and I did not have it before'. Now that seems to me a cause for celebration especially

44

when it was achieved by two human beings who didn't bloody each other. But don't misread Frank, he's a sardonic old bastard.

J.G.   What about about the idea of Charles Laughton as Frank in 'Educating Rita'?

W.R.   Yes, that's how I saw the character and I still do. I was very interested in offering it to George Melly. Obviously George can act, but I don't know if George would have been remotely interested. Laughton always called himself a supremely ugly man who achieved beauty through the level of his performance and I in a sense wanted Frank to be like that so there would be no question of sexual engagement between the two of them. Which is, I suppose, why I had Laughton in mind, because if you looked at Laughton patently there's going to be nothing between them. Now that shows you what absolute folly an author can bring to his own work, because the play would not have had a lot of its electricity if the audience hadn't been able to sit there thinking well, are these two going to - you know what I mean? I hadn't foreseen that.

J.G.   Can we talk a little bit about Frank? Is there a particular man that he is based on, in your own experience, because he's a failed academic who has lost touch with his own creativity?

W.R.   No, I can't think of any figure in life who influenced Frank. He's a sort of straight-out-of-the-air creation but he does share again the thing that a number of characters have in the plays of being, to my mind, a real teacher, i.e. he provides the space and the stimulus in which somebody can securely learn, and that's what he does for Rita. And the other thing is, don't forget that working in Frank's voice, I was able to write a lot of things in a certain way that I couldn't perhaps write in other idioms, in other accents. There are certain ways of thinking that an 'educated' man will have, that I was able to deal with for the first time in a play, most of which I share. In a sense you can see Rita and Frank as two sides of Willy Russell.

J.G.   Do you share his sense of disillusionment with the standard academic curriculum because it excludes good, modern work?

W.R.   Yes. You know how most academics in institutions lag painfully behind what is happening in the real world of life. How many courses are there that debate Tom Wolfe and Martin Amis? I am not saying that they should. In Germany, for example, my work and the work of contemporary English dramatists is widely studied, and has been for a long time. You try and find the equivalent situation in an English university, you'd be pretty hard pressed. There's an academic world and there's a writing world. Writers are very different from academics but often it's academics who become the spokespersons for the writers and, therefore, the writers are often terribly mis-represented, but most of us ultimately have not got any desire to go and talk about ourselves in that way and our work, so we leave it up to other people to get on with it, so maybe we have the situation we deserve. And, as I was saying before, when analysis starts to obscure the work itself, then it is not fulfilling its function. I was interested in David Lodge's recent statement that he thinks the study of English literature is basically decadent, and there is still a feeling, and this is to parody it almost, but there is a feeling that if a work exists contemporaneously and is popular, then somehow it is not for the universities.

J.G.   Going back to your own time as a school teacher at Dingle Vale, was that influential in the sense of developing your playwriting, because you held the attention of the toughest kids in the school by telling them stories in a real scouse accent? In other words, you would tune into their idiom. Did you learn from that?

W.R.   I did learn from that. I mean, basically what happened was I had this class called 4WD, and it was the first year the school had become comprehensive in name. In fact, it was three different school sites, so politically it was a disaster, tribally it was a disaster because in those areas the kids didn't want anything to do with each other. It was also the first year of the raising of the school leaving age, so we had a terribly resentful fourth year who were going to have to stay on till they could leave at Easter when they were 16. Now it was decided that Dingle Vale boys and Dingle Vale girls should be segregated and so we had a fourth year that included some all boys classes and it was decided that the problems were such that rather than try and integrate them at this late stage in their education, we might as well just grit our teeth, leave them as solo boys classes and solo girls classes and one of these was 4WD. And 4WD had one period a week with me and I was a probationary teacher there. I never thought to wonder why they only had one session a week. I walked in the first day of the first week, to see all the light bulbs shattering on the floor because they had unscrewed them and as I came through the door, threw them up in the air. They were sitting there innocently with folded arms as the light bulbs exploded, and I thought 'Oh, terrific'. Now even as a very young teacher I could hold a class and I had no problems with communication, creating the right sort of environment but I couldn't with 4WD; there was a resistance that was unbelievable. I mean the noise level was just incredible. On the timetable it said English and Drama, so in that first week I tried to give out some paper, tried to get them to write something; 'Sir, we haven't got a pen, Sir, we haven't got a pencil'. By the time I'd sorted that out the bell went, it was gone and it was a terribly miserable half hour for me. And this started to play on my mind, because I just couldn't get my hook into this class at all. I went in the next week and it was even worse, I never even got to the point of giving out the paper and they were really quite hard. You couldn't rely upon any sort of assumed respect for the role of teacher. I'd had difficult classes as a probationary teacher and in my teacher training but I had never had anything that was as schizophrenic and as fractured as this; there was no centre to it, that was the weird thing. And, of course, they'd be ruthless in their racism; there wasn't even any sort of

46

vestige of collective liberalism you could appeal to. There was a Chinese kid, they just used to call him a Chinese twat and that was that. I mean, if he held up a pencil they'd whack him around the head, snatch the pencil out of his hand and if he complained, boot him. It was as animalistic and it was as brutal as that. In other classes if an incident happened like that within the class it would be an isolated incident involving two or three kids at most. The consensus in this class was that that was absolutely the right way to behave. You didn't have anywhere to start, and it was almost like a sort of forest fire situation. Obviously when this Chinese boy got abused like that, I'd move in and I'd say,'Eh' and they'd back off because I had used a straight forward non-liberal voice like 'I'm actually bigger than you'. You don't say that, but you walk up and go 'Eh' and they back off. You'd then be thinking 'I'm going to have to knock shit out of this kid'. It really was a terribly, terribly complex situation to try and deal with. I thought 'Don't be the liberal here; you are actually causing that Chinese kid more problems' and you could see it in his eyes, he was almost saying to you 'Piss off'. If you stay away from this situation you won't blow it up into anything big, and at the end of the day, I'll be away from them and I won't have anything to do with them, so there was all that complex stuff that any teacher has to face highlighted by the nature of this particular class. But anyway, this started to play rather heavily on my brain and I was getting more and more miserable. Having to go in every week to this, it was becoming intolerable. I'd finished the one half hour session on a Thursday and the first thing to think about is this class rolling around again and next Thursday was on the horizon, so I wasn't enjoying anything I was doing and my bottle was starting to go, privately. Because I felt there was some great failure on my part. I mean, one of the things I didn't think to ask about, was why had I, a probationary teacher got this infamously difficult class, when they were split up right across the board. Nobody had them for more than half an hour a week, that's why I only had them for half an hour a week. Even the most experienced teachers wouldn't have them for more than half an hour a week. And the other probationary teachers didn't get them at all. So I wasn't failing, but I didn't know that at the time. Or, like I say, I was failing along with everybody else. Anyway, this started to prey on my mind. I think I must have read an article in The Guardian about a teacher in New York somewhere down in an area like Queens and he reported how he had a situation which seemed very similar to mine, totally broken down. What he did was he walked in one day and he took the newspaper in with him and sat down at his desk and opened the paper and he started to read it. The noise got worse, the screams got worse, the abuse and a huge punch up occurred every week until after weeks and weeks of this eventually they came to him and said, can't we do something? He put the paper down and that was the starting point. I always knew that you could use theatricality in teaching but I often wasn't brave enough to do it, because you don't half expose yourself. Because all the best teachers I ever had, like Harry Armstrong, were intensely theatrical performers. One thing I had learned from a teaching practice in Halewood, is that when you have a mob situation on your hands or a completely unruly class, you don't try to supersede their vocal levels, because all you succeed in doing is pushing up the entire vocal level. There was a girl who was teaching a class next to me when I was a student teacher and I used to cringe at what was happening to her voice box because she kept getting higher and higher in volume and pitch, and the kids just were able to go effortlessly up with her and she was shredded. So I knew that when you had a situation like that, the fatal thing was to go in and try and shout louder than them. I went in to 4WD this day and it was cacophonous as usual, and I sat at the desk, and just started to tell a story like 'then these children sat on the wall talking and kicking the wall and this woman came out and she said "Get off my wall" so they shrugged and moved'. Sure enough the noise level subsided and started to go - I wasn't doing anything, I wasn't looking at them, I wasn't holding a book to read from but they started to listen to what was going on and I don't know what hooked them so fast, but hook them it did. Half an hour later the bell went and they all stormed out, knocking over desks as usual. But I knew I'd got them, I knew I'd hooked them. I went in the week after and they were all sitting there and said 'Going to have that story again, aren't we?' I said 'Which story?' 'That fucking story you told us last week'. And you knew you had them, then, so I just carried on, making up this long, long story about two kids who try and run away to Wales, and it went on and on and on. I felt guilty about this, I felt I was getting by but I wasn't teaching them, you see. Because I was making the great mistake of thinking all teaching can only be teaching if somehow they write about it, if we can quantify it in some sort of way. One day I get into the staffroom and this teacher says to me 'I'm coming to your lesson today because I have to report on you as a probationary teacher'. I said 'Which one are you coming into?' He said 'I thought of coming into 4WD'. He said 'I'll give you five minutes to start the lesson and I'll come in'. So I went in and I took a load of paper and pencils in and said 'Listen lads, I've been telling you this story now for like the last ten weeks but today I'm being examined by a geezer so would you mind if we wrote something about it?' They could see the justice in the situation as it were, because I was asking them, I suppose, to get involved in a bit of a scam on my behalf. But for some reason, I changed my mind and started to tell them the story again. This teacher came in, I didn't look at him, I kept my eyes off him, until just before the end of the lesson, I looked up and he was sitting at the back with his thumb in his mouth, as lots of these kids did when they were listening to the story, they went back to the infant stage of putting their thumb in their mouths, and he was doing the same thing. It was a break immediately after that lesson and this teacher told me it was the best lesson he'd ever come across. And I realised that he was bit of an off the wall teacher, so I still didn't value it, because he was off the wall like me. He said the level of interaction for those kids was incredible. So at least I could go on doing it, which I did. I mean, I never did any other lesson with this group, all the way through till Easter, when they left. And, of course what I realised years later was that I had stumbled on to something that was really, really important, the nature of oracy as opposed to literacy, the nature of story telling and the fact that working class kids responded to that because I was working in their language - I mean that literally and metaphorically, the language that their culture is carried in, you see. Obviously I had the talent and the theatrical capabilities, the skills to carry that off; in less qualified hands it could have proved disastrous. A long time before I did think of an idea for a play and it came out of the teaching practice experience. You know what it's like when somebody has a bad teaching experience, all their instinct goes and they seem to exacerbate their own situation. They start trying to work all night on lesson plans so they go in tired, and then they get desperate and self-conscious. Teaching is like sex really, the more conscious you become of it, the less good you are going to be at it. It is one of those things that takes a certain - well, like acting, it takes a certain jive, you have to get on with it, fly at it. I just thought of this bizarre play in which this student teacher resorts to more and more desperate theatricality to try and grip the kids. Like there's a day when he's got this 4WD class and suddenly the door just opens and Batman leaps in and says 'Right, now write about that!' and they go 'Aagh!'. And he gets more and more desperate till one day he walks in with a gun. And we realise actually he's gone nuts. He's got the loaded gun and he shoots the class dead. And I think in a sense me launching into this thing with 4WD was an element of resorting to a theatricality that would immediately grab them and then it was up to me to hold them, which I could do, whereas this character in my yet-to-be-written play only had the theatrical gesture and then nothing to follow it up, you see.

J.G. Did you make up the story using the kids in the class as models?

W.R. No, I didn't. I created archetypes that they would immediately recognise.

J.G. Is that one of the secrets of your success? The creating of an archetype that people can relate to?

W.R. I think it is the secret of all successful drama. Why is Willy Loman possible, and rich as a character? Not because he is a stereotype, although lots of what he does is stereotypical. More importantly than that he is an archetype, so he speaks to us at a belly and heart level as well as a mind level.

J.G. So in your plays there's a very specific location and setting for the play in, usually Liverpool, but the central character has an archetypal, human significance. And it just comes out instinctively?

W.R. Yes, it's instinctive, but you know, when I am in the process of trying to write a new play, I will sometimes start things on paper and I won't finish them because my instinct will tell me that it's no good. Other playwrights might want to write it, maybe I should write it but I don't. It doesn't echo back to me. It doesn't have the right sound, it doesn't have the right hallmark, I don't recognise something there that is archetypal, then I don't pursue it, I don't like

49

having to explain a character.

J.G.. Shall we talk about 'Our Day Out'? That's the play that was written very quickly based on your own experiences.

W.R. Well, yes, it was. It took about four days to write it but I had taken a long time thinking about it. I'd tried it a few times when I was still too close to teaching I think, to have that necessary objectivity. And then I was in London in an apartment which Robert Stigwood had hired for me and the family when I was writing the screenplay of 'John, Paul, George, Ringo ... and Bert' and visiting us one night were Michael and Margaret and a couple of other people and Sheila and Jackie, two girls who were at St Katherine's with me, who used to share the same dayroom with me and they'd been teaching for about 18 months and I hadn't seen them for a year. I was then out of teaching. And during the course of the evening, I began to tell tales of the day I went on a school trip with Dorothy King, and I suddenly realised that I had liberated myself from the actuality of it and I was telling tales that I could edit, amplify, and I knew then, that this could be a play one day. But even then, it was another six months before I actually tried it. I tried it a few times and got it wrong and I just hit the right tone this day, so I just stuck with it for four days and wrote it. The film was written solo but then Bob Eaton, who was then director of the Everyman, where I used to have my office, came in one day and said 'We'd like to do a musical in conjunction with the Youth Theatre of ''Our Day Out'''. I said 'Well, it's very interesting you should say that because I'm at work on ''Blood Brothers'' now but I've long had it in my head.' In fact I'd written to Paul McCartney about six months before asking him did he want to come in and compose the music of 'Our Day Out', because I was sitting on a perfect musical plot, with an in-built chorus, principal, sub-principals - it had staging difficulties but I was going to do it after 'Blood Brothers' as a very big, high production value musical. So I said to Bob 'As soon as I get ''Blood Brothers'' finished, I'll do it.' Well of course, I gave him a vague date and, as I said, 'Blood Brothers' rolled on for a year, rather than three months and what happened was, Bob came in and he was desperate because his date was coming round, they'd pushed it forward and pushed it forward, and I think he was about to leave the theatre and it'd never be done. So he said to me 'Look, why don't you let us workshop it?' 'No,' I said 'No way.' I mean, I hate that idea, I could see it being a complete and utter mess but he was desperate so I reluctantly came to a compromise and told him I would spend some time working on it with him and that he and Chris Mellors could come in as collaborators. I would specify where the music would be, what sort of songs they should be and all that. Well, it eventually ended up with me having to come back from 'Blood Brothers' rehearsals for two days, Bob came round to the house and we opened up the script. For example, 'I'm in love with Sir', I had that idea, so it was written. We lobbed in an old song from my folksong days and I said to Bob 'Look, I think it should start with them all singing the idea of ''Our Day Out''. Because we've got to find a way to stage this thing and bring them all on.' So Bob went away that night and wrote 'Our Day Out.' And I'd throw in a couple of verses and then I said 'Briggsy should sing the instructions for how to enjoy a good day out.' Bob and Chris, I don't know which of them, wrote it and then I'd say 'Right, there - Boss of the Bus - Right - Give me a solo moment.' So Bob went away and wrote 'The Boss of the Bus' in a matter of minutes. I then came back to rehearsals and it was amazing, I mean I had said to Bob 'Right, here the feeling should be why can't it always be this way?' I'd come back and just go 'Why can't it always be this way?' and lines like 'I would wash his collars really clean', I remember sitting in the kitchen saying 'That's the sort of thing '. Bob was amazing, he just took any lines that I was giving him and he married them into the song beautifully. I think looking at it the other night it could still stand the sort of job that I was talking about doing on it. There are moments in which it is really musically weak and it could benefit from a really good look at but, the chances are that if you did that you could really damage the charm of it. It does have an innocent charm to it that reflects the way in which it was written. Anyway, what happened then was I came to rehearsals and there were hints of things that we put in that were not developed, so before it was published I did sit down with the script and I applied myself to the observations on the coach which crippled me the other night, had me in tears. I did it in a rather scatty travelling, rhyming structure and we'd had the boring girl just once, so I developed the boring girl all the way through. I tidied it up a bit. But it could still do with a look at, and it might be worth it one day. But then, you cut it off from the very people who I wanted to be able to play it: Youth Theatres, Schools Groups, Rep Companies. There is a terrible dearth of plays, Youth Theatres have been into improvising for so long and what they've not done is throw up writers. Very sad that, I think. But what it does is it provides another play in that very thin list of plays that are do-able by large groups of youngsters. There's 'Zigger Zagger' which now is dated I'm afraid, 'Oliver', 'Grease', 'Blood Brothers' - but it's not available any longer because of the West End - 'Our Day Out' and I'd start to flag now in the plays you can actually do that have meaning for the age of kids that are playing them. I'm not talking about kids dressing up in Tudor frocks, but plays that have some meaning for them.

J.G. Would you re-write the explicit political bit in 'Our Day Out' if you were writing the whole thing now? Would you make it less explicit?

W.R. No, I think every word of it rings true but I think I would develop it more. I'd probably also find a way to dramatically weave it more into the fabric of the piece instead of stopping the play in order to have the platform confrontation.

J.G. What responsiblity do you feel for your audience?

W.R. You've got a great responsibility and one should never bore them, that's a great, great sin. And once they've delivered themselves into your hands, which is effectively what an audience does, you have got great responsibility and they'll let you take them on a most horrendous roller coaster ride, they'll let you terrify and disturb them, and worry them, and challenge them but within a security. There is this sort of unconscious pact, you know, and if you betray that, they'll get off the roller coaster and they won't come back. One of the things in the 60's and 70's was to break down and remove that pact, and actually confront the audience head on and by so doing, terrify most people like me who were sitting there in the audience, because they had taken away my audience role and turned me into an individual, who was part of the production and that wasn't the contract. So you've got to be very careful with the audience relationship. One does harm them, wound them, but within the security of the contract.

J.G.   Can you gauge an audience's reaction to your plays?

W.R.   An audience, for example, which a play is missing will move down in its seat. I mean, literally, everyone of them will actually try and hide from what is happening on the stage. An audience that is engaged will be really alert and bobbing forwards. When we started to do 'Shirley Valentine' at the Vaudeville I used to stand at the back of the circle sometimes, and a lot of light used to flood into the circle so we could see basically the whole of the audience and in Act I, if you saw men with women there as couples, you would see a situation where the woman tended to be really engaged and the man was not - and then we started to notice one night that by Act 2 they were more and more together and terribly sort of intertwined. It tended to have a healing effect. Men at first thought they were going to get bashed to bits but people came out more healed than wounded. But it's not an exact science, it's not a survey. I mean, unless you engage in an individual debate with every member, how can you find the drift of an audience? You just have to have an instinct for it, and engage it. It is very easy to see when they don't like it, very easy to see.

J.G.   Do you get a lot of feedback about your plays?

W.R.   They go to supper and they argue violently for weeks about whether Shirley Valentine stayed in Greece, or whether Rita went to Australia. I do get letters like that. One came on Thursday: 'Can you settle an argument between a friend and I over Shirley Valentine?'; the arguments rage, you know. So they do have their forum and I think it's better that it takes place in that more real world of life itself than in the strained atmosphere of theatre, because you know what happens if you try to have a debate; you tend to have the same questions, actually, arising all the time, from the people who don't mind contributing to the question time. And probably people with fascinating things to say are never heard.

J.G.   Does satire appeal to you?

Willy Russell at the Liverpool Playhouse at the launch of the campaign to save the theatre from closure,
Spring 1991.

W.R.   Satire is what closes on Saturday night, as George Kauffman says. It doesn't work. I hate satire. I find it tedious, maybe because I've never seen any particularly good satire. Give me an example. Lenny Bruce? Lenny bores me. I love the idea of him as a man but ...

J.G.   The great satirists of literature, like Juvenal and Swift are really quite savage in attacking the vices of their time. It seems that often you affirm the importance of the human spirit. You are not a destructive writer.

W.R.   No, I am not. I often get ideas that I would never write. As I say, I could watch others do them, but I wouldn't want to spend three months writing some of them. To plot the descent of man into the evil swamp and the sewer is actually terribly easy to do because we are so near that evil sewer all the time. I mean, one of the ideas I toyed with but I never wrote is a classic example of this; it foreshadowed Tom Wolfe's <u>Bonfire of the Vanities</u>. I had an idea for an apocalyptic piece about a businessman in Liverpool who is at the top, but who because of something begins to fall, and you know how ruthless that world is, it is actually almost like starving in Hollywood - one slip - and I actually thought, I want to go from there to ending with him in the streets of Toxteth with the rioters throwing petrol bombs at riot police. I can understand that descent but I just don't want to show it, because it seems to me patently obvious anyway.

J.G.   What are your views on political theatre?

W.R.   You'll only get to people if you engage them; if you don't win their heart and soul no amount of hectoring, no amount of presenting brilliantly-considered political theses, will win them over. When I was at a conference a few weeks ago, part of the debate was, why has political theatre waned so dramatically in England, when in the 60s and 70s it was rife. Sad to say I kept my mouth shut and put up with most of the twaddle that was uttered for about an hour on the subject. The fact of the matter is that most of it was appalling theatre and that's why we've moved away from it, it was more political than it was theatre and for me that's the wrong way round. You have to start with theatre and, anyway, I have a great belief that anything that is good artistically is political by its very nature. I think 'The Importance of Being Earnest' was political insomuch as it made the world a better place by the fact of its presence. Some plays which addressed themselves to political issues in the 60s and 70s made the world a worse place because they were pieces of bad work that demoralised the audience. With regard to my own work, I always think of it as being political, but political more in a philosophical than a party political sense. For example, when Rita steps on to the university campus, it's an immense political act for her, and of course it was recognised as such by thousands of other women. And when Shirley decides to take a fortnight's holiday in Greece, in her world that

54

is a massive political gesture. I have been through some of the worst evenings ever in the theatre under the guise of 'political theatre' and it has left, I think, in our generation a very bad taste in the mouth, so we don't really want a great deal to do with it. Don't forget in St Martin's Lane recently there was a carnival of destruction under the banner of a political act. I mean, a mob went insane. Outside 'Blood Brothers' a guy in a Porsche was stopped by a mob who turned the car over with him in it and started to try and set fire to the petrol tank, with him in the car. Now I have to say that during the 60s and 70s there was some of that thinking, as radical as that, involved in the political theatre movement. A lot of us have got older: political we may be, evil we are not.

J.G.   How significant is class in your plays? I remember one interview you gave when 'Blood Brothers' was opening in London, you were in the dressing room with Barbara Dickson and the interviewer asked what the play was about, and you said, 'Well it's about what most of my plays are about, which is class.' Does that statement still stand?

W.R.   No, because I think it's about other things as well, but I have had the benefit now of many years being able to watch it and see that it engages on other levels, so it is about guilt, as much as it's about class. Shirley is of a definite class. Again very consciously I set about writing a piece of work which presents a woman confronting her destiny in Europe, the Henry James classic theme. I'd read Hotel du Lac using that theme in a contemporary way. There have been films on this theme which I was aware of, and I'd stumbled again on to an archetypal story. The solo traveller, going into foreign lands. I don't want the audience to know that, I don't show it off, I'm not going to make allusion to Henry James, but it's a comfort for me when I am writing and it gives me a strength that I'm connected with that archetype, I suppose. I did understand that up to twenty-five years previously, it would have been impossible for Shirley Valentine to have gone on that journey because as a woman in a working class marriage, even though class is not spouted about in the play, she would not have been able to travel abroad. Because the working classes did not have European travel then. So, even when the plays are not so consciously addressing class, it underpins even the plot of it. So, yes, it is important to me, but increasingly I do see that there are very definite tribes of people in our society and I find that more intriguing. And especially as now it is becoming very confused anyway, because what we are starting to develop in this country, along with some of the countries of Europe, is a very entrenched underclass. It is more and more difficult to talk about any working class. Don't tell me that there is not a working class/middle class divide in this country, because there is. Now I won't get on a soap box and spout about it, if you don't say to me it doesn't exist; if anybody says to me it doesn't exist my hackles will rise and I will start pointing out to you graphically how it does exist in our society, but I don't want to shout about it in my plays. I don't live my life self-consciously worrying on behalf of a deprived, dispossessed class. But the fact is that my sympathies are inevitably with a group of people, a section of society who've drawn the short straw. That's all there is to it. I'm not saying that I like them as people more than I like the people of the middle classes, what I am saying is - these are the people who drew the short straw. Let's address ourselves to that fact.

J.G.   Is 'Blood Brothers' then your favourite work?

W.R   No, I don't have a favourite work.

J.G.   Is the most important work the most recent work or the one you are about to do?

W.R.   I wouldn't be disloyal to any of them by saying that one was my favourite, like children. You like each of them, for particular characteristics they have and to elect a favourite would be to consign the rest to a secondary position and I could never do that.

J.G.   How influential is the role of your wife in your writing, does she give you her approval?

W.R.   She's very approving, she's very influential.

J.G.   You were talking about Ibsen, a lot of the strong, independent women in his plays apparently are based on his own wife.

W.R.   No, Annie has never been a model for a character, not remotely, the characters are very, very different to her. But she does have an influence because she is a very good critic, in the best sense of the word. She will look at a scene, she will listen to a scene, a lyric, or whatever, and she will give her opinion as to why it works or doesn't work, so I can enter into quite robust debates with her, so she is influential in that way rather than in the area of character formulation.

J.G.   She must have been quite an influence at an early stage. It was very fortuitous that she had a cultured background.

W.R.   Absolutely.

J.G.   She was the perfect person for you to meet at that particular time, wasn't she?

W.R.   Yes, there was no doubt that was very fortuitous to move into that world and to see other possibilities, and to move amongst people who took the sort of thing I was trying to do seriously.

J.G.   So the Seagroatt family have had an important influence on you, particularly at that early stage. Is that fair enough to say?

W.R.   Yes.

J.G.   What role did your own parents play, or is it a case of you rebounding against their expectations for you?

W.R.   No, the problem is if you specify, it is easier to describe and specify the influence of the Seagroatts than it is to describe the influence that my own parents had. Don't forget, one should always bear this in mind, I was writing and performing before I'd met Annie, or Michael and Margaret so in a sense, the talent influence I think came from my parents, whereas the influencing of how to develop that talent came, I think, in part from the Seagroatt family. It was a question of the informal and then the formalising. That synthesis, one is useless without the other.

J.G.   Were Annie and the Seagroatt family very influential in encouraging you to go back into education, for example?

W.R.   Yes.

J.G.   I know you were desperate to get out of education at 15 or 16 and then desperate to get back in.

W.R.   When I met them, I was studying traditional music, its roots, its culture and forms. So I'd already begun again the process of informal study. I can't remember how it came about, but I think I decided I wanted to try and get back into a college situation and somebody suggested that I should try doing 'O' level literature. And I tried it.

J.G.   And was it a terrifying experience for you, getting back into education?

W.R.   At first it was, yes; I since recognise this in people who join Open University Arts and Foundation Courses. They feel that they've been shut off from the academic world and they go back into the school situation again, and relive with horror their time at school. So I went through a little bit of that at first but soon relaxed and got into it.

J.G.   You wanted Kate Fitzgerald to be the original Rita?

W.R.   No, there was a bit of a mistake about this - I wanted Julie to do it originally. I was at the R.S.C. and we couldn't just bring in who we wanted and so we had to cast from the R.S.C. - so I said 'Oh well, fine, Kate' who was playing in 'Once in a Life Time', 'Let's go with Kate' and, I'm not sure, but they wouldn't release her. And then they set up 'Nicholas Nickleby' and they couldn't give it to anybody from their entire company. So we cast both parts from outside the company.

J.G.   Let's talk about the background to the writing of 'One for the Road'. How much of you is there in the character of Dennis?

W.R.   There's a fair amount actually, yes. It's a play that I never felt particularly strongly disposed towards. Because it felt to me very much like a technical exercise. It really was me trying to write a play with four characters, and off-stage characters and all that. It's bit heartless, I think, as a play. A bit mechanical. I don't think it 'fits in' really.

J.G.   But are the characters of Jane and Roger based on anyone you know?

W.R.   I think the genesis of it was in Scotland, where I often was in those days, for the New Year with my wife and first child. A lot of us who were musicians used to meet up in Edinburgh for the New Year, be there ten days, play a lot of music and drink a lot of booze. But of course as we got older, so people got married, had families, moved to different areas, so the Edinburgh thing stopped happening. But Davy Parker, one of the guys, moved up to Aberdeen with Mari, a friend of Annie's that he'd married. He was a helicopter technician for Bristow's, and they lived on a fairly up-market, purpose built executive housing estate. We stayed up there with them and, of course, we got to know certain of the neighbours that they'd got to know over the short period they'd all been there. And, on New Year's Eve itself, it got to about three in the morning - you know what happens is you wander out with your bottle of Scotch and, if you are a musician you take your instrument with you and you tend to go first-footing from house to house. You don't know where you are after a bit, especially on a fairly anonymous estate like that. But this particular year was the first year we had Robert, so Annie, who would normally keep going with me, at about three o'clock said 'Look I'm going to go home with the baby and get my head down and I'll see you later.' So that was fine and Mari, Dave's wife, said about half an hour later 'I'm going back to join Annie, I'll see you later.' So me and Dave carried on and we went from this house to that house, to another house - playing for our whisky, as it were. We'd do a few songs and other musicians would join us and drop out. But it wasn't like Edinburgh where this situation was normal because this was happening on this estate where there's a sort of middle-classness that's very brittle. There's a lot of competitive stuff going on about who earns what at what level. So, I suppose we were a bit odd really - anyway, we got back to the house about 8 o'clock in the morning and there, in the kitchen, was one of the women in whose house we'd been at some point during the night, called Rosemary. Really quite an attractive woman. And we walked into this kitchen, me and Dave Parker, who's one of those big, gentle, jolly men, with a grin when he's drunk that goes from ear to ear. He just seems to grin wider, you know. And we'd had a great old roaring, singing, boozy night. But this woman had taken it upon herself to go round to wake Mari up at 7.30 and then start whipping up some sort of hysteria about our anarchic behaviour during the night. Now, poor Mari didn't see it as anarchic at all, but she felt she had to go along with this lunatic neighbour because she wanted to cast it in such a light. Annie didn't get up at all. So we got in and Mari was in tears, this woman had taken over the house and was giving us down the banks for our appalling behaviour. And Parker just grinned more and more and slid down the cabinets and I just said to her 'Bollocks, on your bike' and went through. And yet it all stayed with me because I felt that there was some terribly fierce sexual jealousy at work. It was to do with the fact of these two young anarchists coming in and behaving in this bacchanalian manner, and because of respectability, she couldn't behave like that, but really felt she was the sort of woman who should have been out there with us. Now, I could be quite wrong but it never left me, so obviously there was something going on there. I don't know what it was, but that firm impression was with me. So a few years later, when I came to write 'One for the Road', I had written Dennis, who obviously was an anarchic, disruptive character, and the doorbell rang. I opened the door and who walks in but this woman from all those years ago on this estate. So that's where the play came from. But I think 'One for the Road' really is the most workmanlike of my plays, and I think the reason I rewrote it so much was because of that and I think it shows. I have seen it played well, but there are other plays of mine which really can get by even in terrible productions. 'One for the Road' can't. If 'One for the Road' is not being played by very skilled, light, adept people then I think its weaknesses scream out.

J.G.   In the latest London production was it you who spotted Russ Abbott and thought he would make a good Dennis.

W.R.   Yes, I did.

J.G.   And is that the way you work, if you see an actor or actress and you think that person might work well in my play?

W.R.   Well, it was Bob Swash who wanted to revive the play. Bob had done it originally on tour and tried to get it to the West End but couldn't at the time. And yet his affection for the play had never dimmed and so there was a period in which, after 'Blood Brothers', we weren't doing anything and we were in a caff one night and he said 'Look, I really would like to revive "One for the Road" and do it in town.' So I said 'Well, do it but if you do it, Bob, you know you are taking a risk. I really would try and put a star in the centre of it.' And Bob then said 'Fine, who?' And we discussed various people and then I saw something Russ did on the tele - a sketch, and I thought 'Oh, I think there's an actor there as well as a comedian'. And so we met with Russ and he said 'Yes, I can do it in two years' time.' So we said, 'Fine, we are not in any rush. We've got work to do.' And then the two years came round and Russ came in

59

and he did it and I think it was fine and what have you, but it didn't do sensationally well, I think probably because people who wanted to see Russ Abbott, didn't want to see a Willy Russell play and people who wanted to see a Willy Russell play did not want to see Russ Abbott. I think it was a sort of prejudice there, which one couldn't foresee. Because Russ worked terrifically and he was smashing, a joy to work with, very dedicated. Russ has got such a sort of relaxed charm.

J.G.   I'd like to talk about 'Daughters of Albion', which is one of my favourite plays. What's the background to that?

W.R.   Straightforward. I had to write a play for Peter Willes. What happened was, I was badly advised by some accountants when 'John, Paul, George, Ringo ... and Bert' happened and I was told to put away X amount of money to pay the tax, which I did. Because I've always believed in being free of all debt, I suppose. So I did that and the tax bill came and I paid off the tax and then at Christmas Eve another tax bill came in for about four grand, and I didn't have anything. I had enough to live on but I did not possess four grand. So I was rather desperate and I thought, well, you have to put on your going-to-work clothes. I went to see Peggy and I said 'Look Peggy, I've got a huge tax bill and I've got an offer from a series called "Rooms", which was a daytime soap, to write ten episodes and it would pay me eight grand, and I could pay off this tax bill'. And she said to me 'I don't want you to be doing this, I will set up a meeting with Peter Willes'. So I said 'What for?' 'Well, he commissions plays'. Again, one of the ways in which Peggy was wonderful. So I went to see Peter Willes, we gabbed and he commissioned a play and he sent half the money in advance and then just as I was about to write it, the programme 'Rooms' collapsed and all the writers had to be paid off their entire contracts. So, I would have had my tax bill paid, four grand over and not had to write a word of it! Willes was a very famous producer; he was the man who first produced the likes of Joe Orton on the screen, but he was also very sort of 1920's, he used to walk around in a hacking jacket, plus fours and a walking cane in Leeds. And so he commissioned a play from me. In the meantime, I had applied for and been offered the Fellowship at Manchester Poly, which again I didn't want to take but that offered four grand, so I really could pay the old tax. I'd taken the Manchester Poly job and the first thing I did when I got there was to sit down at my desk in November, knowing that I had to deliver in the end of December this play for Yorkshire. And I wrote 'Daughters of Albion'. I remember I wrote some bits of it one day and I didn't think it was very good at all, and I stuffed it away, and yet I couldn't write anything else. And I went home one night and I was really rather depressed and Annie said to me 'What's wrong?' and a great friend of mine who's no longer with us, called Johnny Owen was staying the night and they said 'Well, surely you've got something?' I said 'Well, I've got this thing about this girl who's on her way to a party but...' And they said 'Read it to us, read it to us'. So I read it to Annie and Johnny and they both loved it.

60

It's very funny, it can be as simple as that, given the confidence that other people's reaction can give you. I just went in the next day and blammed through it. And what I'd worried about was it seemed to me very plotless, I didn't think I should write a plotless piece but I look back on it now and it seems to be intricately plotted and, of course, what I did was I wrote the 'darkness to light', that was the sort of schemata of the piece. I remember having in my head an image that probably arose from a song I was working on, something like that which never saw the light of day, of a group of girls early on a Sunday morning, obviously refugees from a party, unable to get a bus, walking towards the flats on the East Lancs Road - Sparrow Hawk Flats, on the left hand side, you know, in the distance. The three girls on the sort of road that you wouldn't walk along. And it was just that image really that made me write the play.

J.G.   Going on to the idea of how intricately plotted 'Daughters of Albion' seems to be, the same surely could be said of 'Educating Rita'.

W.R.   'Educating Rita' was plotless, you see.

J.G.   But it could be argued that it's very intricately plotted.

W.R.   I know that because it doesn't have an overall unity, although you see, in my head it did. In my head it had a structure based on academic terms, but that's not obvious. Maybe it's a good thing it's not. And the structure of 'Daughters of Albion' as I say, is just that, the all night party, from dusk to dawn, and what happens in the madness of the night, shifts and patterns, and the collision of those two cultures again. Peggy Ramsay always thought that 'Daughters of Albion' was one of the best things I had ever written and always went on about it and sometimes you can't see something until long after you have written it. But of course, to go back to what I said this morning, in those days TV drama was the central forum. Fifteen million people watched 'Daughters of Albion'.

J.G.   I remember it clearly, seeing it at University, in May '79 just before the general election. Kathleen was like an early version of Rita.

W.R.   She is indeed, yes.

J.G.   Were you writing Rita at that time?

W.R.   Oh, no, no. From Sandra in 'Breezeblock Park', through Linda in 'Stags and Hens', through Kathleen, I obviously was looking to explore this young woman and it was only when Rita came along that I was able to fully look at this girl. But yes, she's there all the way along the line. But she's interesting, Kathleen, I still love her because she's got no humour. She's great. She's just one of those women who's spot on and cuts through everything. She never laughs, terribly intense, serious girl, but wants to know what's going on - I just love her. Very

Liverpool type that.

J.G. What about Linda in 'Stags and Hens', - is there a model for her?

W.R. No, I think it's the same old working through - no, nothing's a direct model for any of those characters.

J.G. 'One for the Road' plays against the expectations of what went on at a dinner party, doesn't it?

W.R One of the things I wanted to do in 'One for the Road' was, I wanted to write a dinner party play under which we didn't have to suffer the dinner party, so that's why I put the dinner in the interval. But the beginning of that play was Dennis, it wasn't really a set. Now the beginning of 'Stags and Hens' was the set. I suppose I'd always wanted to try and set a play in that club-cum-ballroom atmosphere but you can't put 400-500 gyrating bodies onto a stage. You could do that in films perfectly where you can take the camera anywhere but on the stage, it's very difficult to focus the eye and the ear of the audience, when you've a vast company. So it was only when I came up with the idea of putting it in the ladies and gents that I realised I had a play. So, in a sense, that began really from the idea for the set. But I do like to try and be clever with the stage. I mean, there was something in 'Breezeblock Park' which never ever worked really and yet I loved the idea of it - the idea that the house in Act I is merely the reverse of the house in Act II, so that you show immediately that Betty and Renee have cancelled themselves out, they have identical houses. But in fact what happens is the curtain goes up for the second act and I'm sure the audience think that the producers haven't got much money so what they've just done is turned the set round. But it's not glaring enough. It's not like Greece in 'Shirley Valentine' so the joke backfires a bit, I think. But of course the setting of Rita was crucial because the room was another character (which one had to lose when it was filmed).

J.G. Was that a happy coincidence, that your in-laws had a house with a backroom as a study with a desk and the chair and typewriter?

W.R. And mega books - yes, yes, but I was also by that time aware of many other studies. I had my own so I was aware of the womb with a view, as Dylan Thomas called it. Often the problem with writing a play is to find a convincing way in which you can bring the action before the eye of the audience. Now, apply that to 'Stags and Hens'. One solved it by the loos and in 'Rita' one solved it by tutorial rooms. The reason for her coming to that room is implicit, it doesn't look like a stage contrivance. It is, everything's contrived, but it doesn't seem like a contrivance. It is often the most simple things that are the most difficult. With film, of course, you can take the audience's eye anywhere but on stage it is how to find a device, a contrivance whereby you can bring it to the eye of the audience. The same is true of 'Stags and Hens'. Getting people on and off is a bitch and people will never talk about that on writing courses. But you see, on my course they did. And it's crucial.

J.G.   How conscious are you of having to grab the attention of the audience right from the start?

W.R.   Totally.

J.G.   Because I've noticed in 'Rita' and 'Shirley Valentine' the jokes become less and less as the play mines deeper and deeper into the characters and themes.

W.R.   That's true and there's a natural reason for that. It can be explained away in terms of pure naturalism because when Shirley first starts to engage with us, the audience, just straightforward nervousness would mean she cracked more gags. When Rita is very defensive she resorts to humour with Frank; the more confident she becomes, she says I don't want to come to your house and play the court jester. I know I can use my humour all the time but there are times when I might not want to. You see Frankie Howard socially, at a dinner, he never cracks a gag, that's for him at work.

J.G.   Obviously you find it easy to come up with these witty lines.

W.R.   No I don't. I am not a witty man.

J.G.   Do you have to work on that?

W.R.   No, no, I don't work at it, because you can't work at wit. You can't eke it out because it will show. I have occasionally done that, I've striven for a line and my God, does it get cut rapidly in preview because it smacks of construction, of cleverness. But what happens is, if I get the characters right, the wit emerges out of the characters. As I say, I'm not a funny man, I love wit, I love witty people and I really admire them but I am not myself. It's a funny thing, wit, wit demands a real detachment; you can't get caught up too heavily in the content of what is being said and be a wit. You always need to have the detachment, you always need to be listening to what is being done with the language. The best example of this quality is George Kauffman, the American playwright who was one of the famous Algonquin set. He was sitting at the table one day in the Algonquin, and somebody sat down at the table and said 'Had they heard about the appalling fire tragedy in northern Spain in which hundreds of people had died trying to get out of this fire and being crushed in the doors of the hotel as they tried to get out?' And Kauffman just said straight off 'Which just goes to prove you should never put all your Basques in one exit'. To make that line means that you cannot get caught up in the emotion, the picture of these people; so wit by its very nature has a callousness and a coldness

Willy Russell and Noreen Kershaw, the first actress to play Shirley Valentine, March 1986.

Willy Russell and Noreen Kershaw in rehearsal for 'Shirley Valentine'. (Phil Cutts)

Russell reading from 'Shirley Valentine', at the Everyman in 1986. (Phil Cutts)

Russell giving a performed reading of 'Shirley Valentine' at the Everyman.   (Phil Cutts)

Willy Russell signing copies of a poster for the Unity Theatre advertising a performed reading of 'Shirley Valentine' he gave at the Liverpool Playhouse on 4 July 1987.

and a detachment to it. Now I as a human being don't function in that way. However, once I have created a character, the characters for some reason can become witty. I mean, Rita is a terribly witty woman. Shirley is very witty. Some of the girls in 'Daughters of Albion' are very witty. And one has a Liverpool facility for that, it's a way of viewing the world, but it is usually when my characters are at their most defensive that they are being their most witty. I mean, Shirley does it, Shirley uses wit to avoid the pain. She's constantly cracking another gag about it, in order to avoid being self-pitying. And I found when I was writing Shirley that I became witty, because I became Shirley Valentine. All the way through the writing of that play, I found some days I would let her go, I would get home and I would let her go and then it would take me two or three days to get her back and I went through hellish panics, because I couldn't bring her back. It was really interesting to hear Rod Steiger saying the other night, that when he is working on accents, he never, ever stops the accent until the picture is finished. He goes out to dinner, he makes love in that accent because the great problem with an accent is when you stop it, you have to pick it up again and it can be a real bitch. Now it was the same with the writing of Shirley, once I realised that by letting her go, I made it so much more difficult for myself to start again, so I just completely held on to her. I saw the world in terms of Shirley Valentine, so I'd be across at my neighbours having a word with them about something and I'd say things and they'd all be falling about. Because it would be Shirley Valentine talking, - not me and I wasn't doing it in a cynical way, to try stuff out to write it into the play next day, because most of what she said when she was inhabiting me did not go into the play. So I say that with Shirley it was performed as much as it was written.

J.G.   Where did you actually write it, were you at home or here in your office?

W.R.   A strange thing with me is that in order to write a new play, and I only noticed this very late in life when I suddenly saw that there was a very obvious pattern, I have to get away from the place where I am expected to do my writing. I have to go into some sort of hiding. It is not a conscious affectation, it was only something I lately became aware of, that I had never written - begun writing - any play in the place that was my formal writing place. I always began it somewhere else. It is to do with getting away completely from the history of this creature called Willy Russell and becoming again this struggling human being who is trying to write a play.

J.G.   So where was 'Shirley Valentine' written?

W.R.   I began it, I think, in the kitchen and then I wrote a lot of it at home. And then I was able to bring some of it up here. I went next door with it too for the music.

J.G.   And what about 'Blood Brothers'? Where was that written?

W.R. I had an office then at the Everyman but I wrote 'Marilyn Monroe,' the song, on the kitchen table at home in Woolton. We'd just moved out of the house in Newsham Park but which I hadn't sold, and I went there to work every day.

J.G. What about the screen play? Is that different?

W.R. Yes, it's an adaptation, I just do that here.

J.G. Changing tack a little bit, what other writers do you admire? You mentioned Ibsen. Is he a writer that you have taken something from?

W.R. No, not particularly, but what I do when I am coming up to having to write a new play myself, is I tend to wallow in good dramatic writing. I tend to keep reminding myself of the greatness of plays. How great they can be, and how all the great plays are timeless and how there's nothing about my age which isn't true of all ages past because drama itself is totally ageless and so the problems that Ibsen faced and Chekhov faced and Shakespeare faced and Moliere faced, are the problems that I am going to be facing when I have to put their work down and look at my blank paper. And I will see that 'Hedda Gabler' is a play that springs into life because of very basic things. We see on stage there before us an intensely dissatisfied woman and a rather fastidious, pedantic man. Now what's earth-shattering about that? It is as common as muck; a woman who is persuaded to give a baby away - it's all stuff that you might overlook if you fail to see the nature of drama as something which operates at simple levels. I don't mean simplistic at all, not at all. Because simple can mean extremely sophisticated, like the simple pop song, is a thousand times better than the complex pop song. The simple pop song has lasted from 1956 to today and will last for another 'x' years, because it has the beauty and the elegance of its simplicity. The complex pop song, which we all thought would last for a long time in 1966 and we still have a nostalgia for, will die out, because it will die out with us. It is only our nostalgia which keeps it alive. Whereas, 'Roll Over Beethoven', 'Sweet Little Sixteen', 'Cathy's Clown', will last because they have the beauty and the power of simplicity. So that's why I always go back to reading writers who always understood that, and especially writers who have been so widely written about by academics that we are all in danger of being terrified by their reputation. Chekhov was a working dramatist, trying to solve the problem of how to get that character on to the stage at that moment. It's not a spiritual, mystical thing, but obviously in my own way it is something about being back in touch. It could sound terribly arrogant of me to be talking about myself in terms of these writers but I hope it's not. Because I'm not talking about these men who became so elevated through what they did; I am talking about the basic dramatists they were. Now I do feel that I have a true line to those people, and when I sit down - when I've not read them for a while, but I've heard lots of critics talking about them, I can start to feel betrayed by Chekhov and betrayed by Ibsen, and betrayed by Shakespeare, because they've gone off and joined this club with all these academics - but I know really if they were around today, they wouldn't be in that club. They'd be in the same club that I'm in, because they were dramatists. Print that, it's the nearest I've ever got to talking about what it is about making plays.

From 'Keep Your Eyes Down' to 'Terraces': The Plays of Willy Russell

'Keep Your Eyes Down' (1971)

Willy Russell went with his girlfriend Annie Seagroatt to see John McGrath's 'Unruly Elements', an evening of five short Liverpool plays directed by Alan Dossor, at the Everyman Theatre in March 1971. The plays made an immediate impact on him, and Russell decided he wanted to be a playwright. He had been a songwriter for about six years, he'd written poetry, songs and sketches to make people laugh since he was fourteen, he'd even started a novel. But now his interests focused strongly on playwriting. 'Unruly Elements' was the first play he'd seen which related closely to his own life, and did so in a direct, contemporary style of language which was not unpoetic. After seeing McGrath's play Russell realised the direction his writing should take. Up till then, he had suffered badly from 'art in the head', trying to be Philip Larkin or Graham Greene. McGrath's play reconnected Russell to his own working class tradition of storytelling, especially as the language used was Liverpool dialect .

Willy Russell was also frequently attending plays at the Unity Theatre in Liverpool at this time. Unity is an amateur theatre group with a broad repertoire of plays, both classical and contemporary. The first play Russell wrote and considered good enough to produce, 'Keep Your Eyes Down', was submitted to the Unity Theatre on 4th November 1971 but it was rejected by them, although a copy is now in the archive of the Unity Theatre in the Merseyside Museum of Labour History in Liverpool. Russell also submitted it to Alan Dossor, Artistic Director of the Everyman Theatre who was not able to use it, although he enjoyed reading it. Russell was to work closely with Dossor in a couple of years time on projects such as 'John, Paul, George, Ringo... and Bert'.

'Keep Your Eyes Down', a fifty minute play, was first performed at St. Katherine's College by the College drama society on 4th, 5th and 6th December 1971 for the drama course annual production. The Liverpool Echo acknowledged it on Thursday, 9th December with a short article entitled 'Willie makes his debut as a playwright'. He was then a second year drama student at St. Katherine's. 'Keep Your Eyes Down' is a fascinating play mainly because it reveals for the first time Willy Russell's pervasive dramatic vision, an individual's escape attempt from imprisoning circumstances, and his dynamic use of Liverpool dialect. Many of the themes which appear repeatedly in his later, mature work are present in 'Keep Your Eyes Down' such as the search for self-realisation, freedom and choice and peer-group pressure to conform to other people's low expectations. There is a strong sense in the play that the writer has something of real importance to say and possesses a very powerful, individual voice. The play's central character is Smarty whose fate, according to family, friends and employer is to work in a factory for the rest of his life, but he wants fame and fortune in the music business. The problem with this play is its allegorical style. Later, when submitted as a T.V. play, the producer Barry Hanson wrote to Russell advising him to reject the allegory and concentrate on realism. Russell took his advice and re-wrote it as the very fine T.V. play 'The Boy with the Transistor Radio' (1979).

'Blind Scouse' (1972)

The success of 'Keep Your Eyes Down' prompted the college drama group Cateysaints to present the play on the Fringe at the Edinburgh Festival in August 1972. Cateysaints was a company formed from members of the drama society of St. Katherine's College of Education. Most members of the company had worked together previously but this was the first major venture undertaken by the Cateysaints. 'Keep Your Eyes Down' was performed alongside two new Russell plays, 'Playground' and 'Sam O'Shanker' or 'Tam O'Shanter Rides again'. In 'Playground' a group of schoolkids kidnap a teacher while 'Sam O'Shanker' translates Burns's well-loved poem 'Tam O'Shanter' into Liverpudlian terms.

These three plays under the collective title 'Blind Scouse' (no deeper meaning is intended by the title 'Blind Scouse', which is scouse with no meat in it) were first produced at St. Katherine's College in Liverpool on 28th, 29th and 30th June 1972. Willy Russell took the part of the narrator in 'Sam O'Shanker'. The same production was taken to Edinburgh Festival Fringe and performed from August 21st to September 2nd at Rifle Lodge, 32 Broughton Street off Leith Walk. Unity Theatre actor John Craig played Sam.

'Playground' is a compact short play in two scenes with six characters and a realistic style with Liverpool dialect. It takes place behind and in front of a bike shed wall in a Liverpool schoolyard. The play concerns a reject of the school system, Robbo, who takes revenge on an unsympathetic teacher, Mr Taylor, by knifing him. Barrie Keefe's triple bill 'Gimme Shelter' included a play called 'Gotcha' which was very similar in situation and sentiment to 'Playground', which preceded it. Willy Russell saw 'Gimme Shelter' at the Liverpool Playhouse Upstairs. It was also televised and there was a furore when the repeat was banned in 1978 with claims of gratuitous violence and the intervention of Mrs Mary Whitehouse.

'When The Reds' (1973)

Taking 'Blind Scouse' to Edinburgh was a vital step in the career of Willy Russell, because John McGrath saw Russell's work one lunchtime. McGrath told Alan Dossor about it and he went to see the plays the following night. There is a satisfying coincidence here: Russell saw McGrath's 'Unruly Elements' at the Everyman in 1971 and decided to become a playwright, then McGrath saw Russell's 'Blind Scouse' and put him in touch with the Everyman and effectively started his career. Dossor was impressed by the way Russell handled local humour and asked him to adapt Alan Plater's play 'The Tigers are Coming O.K?' for The Everyman Theatre. Willy

72

Russell's adaptation of Plater's play ran from 28th March to 21st April 1973.

The play was renamed 'When the Reds' and was completely rewritten, although there was still a great deal of Plater's work in it. The play's setting was a corner of the Kop at Anfield Football Ground with the green turf in the foreground. The auditorium was transformed with posters, red and white favours and slogans, and the central character, Ray, played by Bernard Hill, gave a fine performance as the dedicated fan chattering away almost continuously. Written in the Everyman Theatre style it contained comedy, music, a strong story line about a local topic, an ensemble style of acting and it had political edge. Russell earned £30 for 'When The Reds', which was his first professionally produced play. Russell adapted Plater's play by translating it into Merseyside terms of reference, transcribing much of Plater's original dialogue and adding a considerable amount of pulsating scouse dialogue and songs. The essence of Plater's script was the theme of seeking and yearning in life. Plater symbolised this yearning by the longing in Hull for First Division Football. The problem for Russell was that whereas Hull City F.C. were losers, Liverpool F.C. are winners. So Russell made the Liverpool fan's expectations greater. Liverpool's Ray is more ambitious for success than Hull's Ray. As Plater wrote in his 'Thoughts on Merseyside Tigers' : 'I think our Liverpool Ray, in any case, would regard any football season a failure if they don't win the League, F.A. Cup, League Cup, European Cup and the Eurovision Song Contest... so that the relative failure, year by year, is only a failure seen against the outrageously optimistic - even arrogant - expectations of their supporters. I'm thinking of the feller who christened his son after the entire Liverpool team... that kind of attitude can only really exist in the Pool'.

'King of the Castle' (1973)

Willy Russell's T.V. play 'King of the Castle' was accepted by the B.B.C. just at the time when he was going up to the Edinburgh Festival in August 1972. It was screened on 12th November 1973 on BBC2 as part of the 'Second City Firsts' series.

'King of the Castle' was the fifth of six drama productions written by amateur or semi-professional playwrights and was part of a search for new talent. It was Russell's first venture into T.V. drama and he was paid about £375 for his work. The series was made at the BBC's Pebble Mill Studios in Birmingham. When he wrote it, Russell was still classified as an amateur playwright and, although it is a very interesting piece of work, it was not a tremendous success because it was cut from its intended length of 50 minutes to 30 minutes and it was broadcast in the week of a Royal Wedding, of Princess Anne to Captain Mark Phillips, and did not receive any reviews. He was lucky getting it sold and produced; he was fortunate that he knew which department of the T.V. network to send it to. He had got to know a few T.V. producers when he was involved with the folk club scene. One, Phillip Donnellan, a producer of documentaries, knew he was writing a play and advised him to send it to Barry Hanson . 'King of the Castle' took three weeks to write. It is set in a Liverpool factory and highlights the problems faced by men doing dangerous jobs. At the heart of the factory is a large, terrifying press and the men who climb inside to service it during use risk their lives and safety rules are ignored. A man nicknamed Brocky (played by Bill Maxwell) had worked on the press for years and enjoys the prestige of being 'king of the castle' in the factory doing very dangerous work cleaning and changing tools under the press, but he develops a morbid fear of being trapped, crushed and killed. In Russell's unproduced play 'The Bent' (c.1973) the central character is killed on a conveyor belt in a factory.

'Sam O'Shanker' (1973)

While he was still teaching full-time, Russell worked semi-professionally as a playwright from 1972 to 1974. He had taken 'Blind Scouse' to the Edinburgh Festival in summer 1972 as an amateur. One of the three plays, 'Sam O'Shanker', was subsequently re-worked for the Everyman Theatre Touring Company, Vanload, with plenty of new dialogue, songs and music. It toured clubs, pubs and community centres on Merseyside from 27th December 1973 for several weeks. It is a very spirited piece of work and reflects the Everyman policy of accessible popular theatre, local subject matter, an ensemble style of playing as well as Russell's growing strength as a writer. 'Sam O'Shanker' has a strong story line, sharp and witty Liverpool dialogue, exuberant songs and a universal theme: the dangers of drink!

Unfinished or professionally unproduced plays

In the early 1970's, a number of Willy Russell's plays were not produced professionally or were actually unfinished. The title of 'Point Eight' refers to the average number of children in a modern family: 2.8 - Point Eight is found in a cupboard! 'Point Eight' was written for and performed at Childwall County College where Willy studied for his 'O' and 'A' Levels. 'Tam Lin' (1972) is a fairy story with a narrator, a Fairy Queen, fairies, an ogre and witches. It was performed at Dovecot Primary School, Liverpool in 1973. 'Man who killed the Motor Car' concerns a fascist takeover of the British Government, caused by serious traffic congestion. Three governments have fallen, unable to solve the problem of the morning rush hour which isn't over before the evening rush hour begins. It is a futuristic play conjuring up a picture of Britain with a smog-filled atmosphere and clogged roads. In 'Breakdown', two workers called Stanley and Simon begin to enjoy themselves when factory machinery breaks down. They remember their boyhoods with nostalgia, and contrast it with their dull, repetitive factory work. The play deals with industrialisation and its dehumanising impact on people. It was rejected by the B.B.C. in 1973. 'Playmates' is about Jack, a disillusioned but successful singer and songwriter and an unknown but talented singer called Sam who eventually takes over Jack's career and takes his girlfriend as well. 'The Bent' (1973) was written for Half Moon Theatre and is based on Shakespeare's 'Coriolanus'. Set in a Liverpool car factory, it concerns Johnny Egan, an idealistic shop steward who becomes disillusioned with his job, his father and the factory workers. He resigns as shop steward, then gets a job with management but is equally disillusioned with them and dies trying to make safe parts of the factory, deliberately neglected by his boss for personal ambition. 'Screwed Down' is an unfinished play written for The Everyman Touring Company in 1973. The action takes place in and around the warehouse and managerial office of Screw Rubber Company, and concerns strike-bound Merseyside industry and the attempts by Prime Minister Heath's agent Kristian Kleen to improve Liverpool. It is the kind of direct, heavy-handed political drama that Russell left behind. 'Lucy Wan' (1973) was not written in scouse dialect unlike most of his other unproduced plays. The original idea comes from a Scots/ English ballad known as 'Lizzie Wan' or 'Lucy Wan'. John and Eve are the ill-matched parents of Lucy and William. They have an incestuous relationship and Lucy becomes pregnant. William realises what he has done is wrong and goes off with another girl, leaving Lucy behind. It is a bleak play, making use of a folk ballad quite effectively. It was rejected by Yorkshire T.V. in 1973.

In 1974 Russell collaborated with Alan Bleasdale on a T.V. script called 'On the Rob' which was a pilot for a possible T.V. series of half-hour plays entitled 'Scully'. 'On the Rob' was Episode 1 and Russell was paid £300 for his work. Russell and Bleasdale also collaborated on 'Sculliver's Travels', a T.V. play about Scully who finds a book about Gulliver's Travels. It concerns Scully's adventures on the way to a pop festival in the Isle of Wight. Scully and his mates hitch-hike down, hoping to meet girls, but when they get there the pop festival is a wash-out and they come back only pretending they've had a great time. Mooey Morgan goes with them but he thinks 'y' fall off the end of the world if y' go past Widnes'. The desire to escape is Russell's favourite story line, however, the characterisation of Scully is Alan Bleasdale's invention not Willy Russell's.

At the time of writing 'When the Reds' in 1973, Willy Russell was teaching at the Dingle Vale building of Shorefields Comprehensive in Liverpool. Ringo Starr attended this school but it had been merged into a Comprehensive since he left. Russell taught English to the toughest class in the school called 4WD. According to one of Willy Russell's ex-pupils from 4WD, Tony While, Russell would enter the classroom and sit at his desk and at first the kids didn't take any notice because they were used to an adversarial teacher-pupil situation. After a few difficult weeks, Russell had the idea of telling them a story and they soon became interested in it. After a time, the kids started to really enjoy his English classes, turning up ten minutes early for them, with kids from other classes coming too on the strength of what they'd heard. The kids identified with the characters in his stories. One of the stories began with 'Last May it was, and it was on the corner, and there were two kids, one called Icky and one called Billy, kicking a ball against the wall'. The saga of Icky and Billy lasted months, and became 'One Summer'', the T.V. play broadcast in 1984. Russell also read books to them like Steinbeck's Of Mice and Men, a novel he was keen on and which anticipates some of the ideas in his plays about people dreaming of acquiring a decent life for themselves. Russell was regarded as a great teacher, having a special rapport with the kids. Other masters would just rant and rave at them, slam books down on the table and leave the room, but Russell's quieter style was effective. He appeared easy going, and would develop a lesson out of casual conversation. Once he used the word 'vagina' and they all exploded with laughter, so he used it again. Russell was one of the teachers these kids respected; they liked him, so were prepared to accept his advice. Russell left Dingle Vale in 1974 after the success of 'John, Paul, George, Ringo... and Bert' in the West End. He also became embarrassed at receiving his teacher's salary considering what he was earning from the Beatles show.

'John, Paul, George, Ringo ... and Bert' (1974)

Willy Russell put himself firmly on the theatrical map in 1974 when he wrote the musical play 'John, Paul, George, Ringo ... and Bert'. He shot from being a schoolmaster in the Dingle to a West End playwright with his name up in lights: it was his first big commercial success. 'John, Paul, George, Ringo ... and Bert' was presented at the Everyman Theatre, Liverpool on 21st May 1974 and ran for six weeks with never an empty seat after the second night. It then transferred to the Lyric Theatre in Shaftesbury Avenue on 15th August 1974, shortly before Willy's twenty seventh birthday. It ran in London for a year and a day and, again directed by Alan Dossor, it won the London Theatre Critics' and the Evening Standard's Awards for the Best Musical in 1974, even though Russell only wrote two original songs in the show. Subsequently there were two national tours and productions in many foreign countries including West Germany in April 1975 and Mexico in February 1977. It was the

Willy Russell outside the Everyman Theatre, Liverpool, March 1986.

Everyman Theatre's greatest box office success, especially as the original cost of the show was a cut-price £1,000. Fourteen thousand seven hundred people attended the Liverpool run.

Alan Dossor had seen a documentary play at The Contact Theatre, Manchester about The Beatles (in which Bernard Hill played John Lennon) and he thought it would be a good idea if somebody adapted that documentary for the Everyman. After seeing it, Russell said he didn't fancy writing such an adaptation but he did want to write a play about The Beatles because he'd been brought up on the story and knew it backwards. Dossor commissioned Russell to write a play, not a showbiz extravaganza. Russell invented the bulk of the dialogue and took the spirit of the events, rather than going through the biographies and press reports and lifting dialogue verbatim. He tried to capture the spirit of the dialogue as he believed it to be. It was commissioned, written and staged within the space of four months. Russell took a relatively short time to write it, compared with his unpublished novel 'In This New Life' which had taken two years. He began the play on 29th December 1973 and it was finished by March 1974. He sketched the scenes out on a journey to Aberdeen.

'John, Paul, George, Ringo and ... Bert' was written for just a four week run at the Everyman. When Russell saw the response after the first night he realised that he, Alan Dossor and the company had stumbled on to something special. They were really surprised at its success and never expected anything like it at all. But it was perhaps the major turning point in his career. After eighteen months' teaching he could now leave the profession and fulfil his dream of being a full-time writer.

'John, Paul, George, Ringo ... and Bert' is an episodic comedy-drama with music and an earthy script. Bert, the narrator, introduces various incidents in the history of The Beatles from the early days, Hamburg, the Cavern, the 'big time' and finally to their break-up. The four actors playing The Beatles mimed songs but Barbara Dickson actually sang, accompanying herself on the piano along with musicians Terry Canning and Bobby Ash. Alan Dossor was able to cast the play just from the Everyman Repertory Company. Bernard Hill played John Lennon, Trevor Eve played Paul McCartney, Phillip Joseph played George Harrison and Anthony Sher played Ringo Starr, while George Costigan played Bert, the faithful fan. The protean cast played several parts each, in fact there were thirteen actors playing forty three parts. For example, in the original Everyman production, Robin Hooper played the Ballroom Manager, Mr McCartney, Brian Epstein, the Designer and the Promoter. This ensemble style of playing had been used at the Everyman in earlier Russell plays such as 'When the Reds' and 'Sam O'Shanker'. Alan Dossor, who had brought this fabulous company of actors together at the Everyman, suggested there should be four actors for The Beatles when speaking, then a band (Stickey George, a Liverpool group) to play their numbers. But Willy Russell didn't agree, thinking this plan would be a disaster. He thought, rightly, with his strong instinct for what will succeed on stage, that 1974 was too near in time to The Beatles, their sound was too well-known. He felt they couldn't accurately recreate The Beatles' sound on stage. Dunfermline-born Barbara Dickson was asked to sing The Beatles' songs. Russell had known her for about five years from the folk music scene. In fact, Barbara had been staying with Willy and Annie Russell when he was in the middle of writing 'John, Paul, George, Ringo ... and Bert'. He'd already said to her that he'd love to write a musical one day in which he could offer her a part, never thinking he was actually writing the very one. It was only about a week later when he was thinking about how they were going to use the music on stage that he thought how wonderful it would be to have a girl, especially Barbara Dickson, to sing The Beatles' songs and play the piano. One Sunday afternoon he rang her and suggested she could sing in the musical. He knew she had a great voice, but outside the folk club scene, no-one else did because she was known mainly for singing traditional Scottish folksongs. She was terrified and said no way could she do it, but Russell persuaded her to come to Liverpool.

At rehearsals for the show Trevor Eve, who played Paul McCartney, complained of being miscast because he is right-handed while Paul is left handed! He watched the film 'Let it Be' at least four times, running bits of it over and over again to study Paul: each eye inflection, gesture and facial expression had to be absolutely right. He also listened to the post-Beatles records, the ones that Paul made on his own. None of the actors had ever seen a live 'Beatle'.

It took the actors two hours to get made up every night. In rehearsals, Tony Sher's imitation nose kept falling off - it was made of mortician's wax! Alan O'Brien, writing in The New Statesman (31.1.75, p.154) thought Sher's 'Lime Street Cyrano' was amazingly lifelike. Sher was already an accomplished make-up artist and had previously given masterly portrayals of Enoch Powell in 'Tarzan's Last Stand' and of Bill Shankly in 'When The Reds' at The Everyman. Bernard Hill as John Lennon was described as maintaining the 'right tone of intelligent sarcasm, spicing his savage retorts with excremental phrases and a throatful of undeleted expletives'. Phillip Joseph, playing George Harrison, succeeded in delivering a suitably downbeat comic performance 'in a vacuous monotone' (The Stage, 30.5.1974).

The play was an explosion of Liverpudlian vitality and used a potent dramatic situation: an attempt to stage a reunion concert by The Beatles at the Philharmonic Hall in Liverpool. The play shows how their talent was developed by Epstein, loved by the fans, and exploited by media and marketing people with an incredible build-up of pressure on The Beatles which led to their disintegration as a group. The play suggests it was the public who destroyed The Beatles by incessant craving made through the media and marketing people. The play consists of about thirty scenes of varying length interwoven with narration spoken by Bert. The music tapes of The Beatles as well as the versions sung by Barbara Dickson at the piano, with back-projected photographs (a device used in 'When The Reds') supported the actors by recreating the atmosphere of Beatlemania, while telling Russell's version of the story: no bland, sentimental piece of nostalgia, it was far too honest for that.

The Beatles reacted to the show in various ways. George Harrison attended the last but one performance, a Saturday matinee in London, but walked out at the interval because everyone kept staring at him which he felt was unfair to the actors. He then sent a message to say he wasn't displeased with the show. John Lennon sent over a few nice taped messages from America to George Costigan, which Russell still has. George Martin, The Beatles' producer, said it was fairly unbearable and uncanny to sit watching the show. Paul McCartney saw some excerpts on an Arts programme called 'Full House'. He thought he had been portrayed mischievously and stopped the show going to America and prevented the film being made.

The screenplay had been commissioned by The Robert Stigwood Organisation in 1975. Pre-production work including casting was well under way when Paul invoked an American law on the invasion of privacy and everything was cancelled. Russell did not object to McCartney doing this, believing he had a right to do so. When Russell was in London in 1977 with 'Breezeblock Park' a reporter from the Sunday Times interviewed him about 'John, Paul, George, Ringo ... and Bert' asking why the film had been stopped. The resulting article contained nothing about 'Breezeblock Park' but splashed a story about McCartney squashing Russell's project. After this, Paul rang Russell and they talked it over. Willy Russell assured Paul McCartney that the play wasn't an attempt to put him down. Two years later, Paul telephoned Russell and invited him up to Scotland for a week. Paul was working in a portable recording studio in a barn. Russell was commissioned by McCartney Productions Ltd. to write a film.

'Band on the Run' (1979)

McCartney wanted Russell to find an angle for a film featuring the then members of 'Wings' including Paul and his wife Linda. So although Paul had objected to 'John, Paul, George, Ringo ... and Bert' he'd obviously liked the writing. Russell spent a week in the studio watching Paul McCartney at work. He decided Paul's earlier song 'Band on the Run' would make a good story line and he wrote a script with Mike Ockrent. Russell invited Ockrent to join him in this project and the two of them went off to Jamaica with their families to write the first draft.

The film, named after the song and the album 'Band on the Run', is about a pop star called Jet who runs away from business pressures and life as a top rock star to go back to his roots. Paul McCartney was to star in it and write all the songs. The filmscript had Jet leaving his band, and his business pressures, by joining an unknown group. Jet is a megastar but gets into trouble having ordered food at a motorway service area as he doesn't carry money. Meanwhile, 'Wings' have been thrown out of a pub-rock situation and meet Jet at a service area and they team up. This was the way McCartney came back into music after the break-up of The Beatles. He toured Britain with his band 'Wings' in an old van, turning up unannounced to perform in small clubs. There was some good natured argument between Paul and the scriptwriters because Paul wanted a happy ending, whereas Russell and Ockrent wanted the hero to go back and sort out his problems. As a story, it has something in common with 'John, Paul,

George, Ringo ... and Bert' in that it concerns the pressures of life as a top rock star. It is also a typical Willy Russell script in that it is about an escape from difficult circumstances to a better life. Perhaps because Paul went to Tokyo and encountered problems with drugs, followed by a change in the members of 'Wings', the film was never made. In fact the script is still sitting on the office shelf at McCartney Productions Limited. Russell was not involved with the disappointing film 'Give My Regards to Broad Street' starring Paul McCartney.

'The Tale of Blind Joe McSweeney' (1974)

After The Beatles musical, Russell's next work for the stage was 'The Cantril Tales', a Christmas extravaganza to celebrate the Everyman Company's first ten years. The writers who had written for the Everyman were invited to write for this show: John McGrath, Ted Whitehead, Bill Morrison, Adrian Mitchell, Adrian Henri, George Costigan and Willy Russell. 'The Cantril Tales' ran at the Everyman Theatre from December 26th 1974 to 25th January 1975.

'The Cantril Tales' was set in an ale house, The Scabby Inn (the Liverpool version of Chaucer's Tabard Inn), the worst pub on the Cantril Farm estate in Liverpool. Arriving outside the pub in the Tardis from 'Dr Who' is Geoffrey Chaucer, author of The Canterbury Tales. He tells the audience that he's been wandering for years, going to many different times and planets in his mission to save mankind by bringing back the Annual Story Telling Competition. Chaucer goes into the pub and persuades the locals to tell their own tales. At the end of the evening the cup is presented to the best story teller and Chaucer disappears in a cloud of smoke, having been denied the opportunity of telling one of his own tales. Russell contributed the first tale called 'The Tale of Blind Joe McSweeney' which concerned a pop star with an aversion to people who pick their noses. Russell also wrote several songs for the show: words and music for 'Chaucer's Travelling Song', 'You Keep on Rocking' and 'Drinking Up Time' and the words of 'The Song of the Superstud'.

'The Death of a Young, Young Man' (1974)

Willy Russell entered a play called 'The Death of a Young, Young Man' for the Radio Times T.V. Drama competition in 1974. It was one of the finalists but didn't win though one of the judges, playwright Hugh Whitemore, praised its 'gentle poetic quality', a slightly odd description considering the violence, both verbal and physical, in the play. It was shown on 30th January 1975 as a BBC1 'Play for Today'. The play was set in farmland overlooked by Kirkby on the outskirts of Liverpool. Some of the filming of bus stops and streets at the start of the play was done in Kirkby, but most of the filming was actually done in the Midlands around Sutton Coldfield. BBC Pebble Mill, H.Q. of English Regions Drama said it was cheaper to do it that way. The play draws on Russell's own experience of potato picking, and concerns three Liverpool lads, aged about fifteen, at a loose end after being suspended from school. Cazza was played by Andrew Schofield, Bo by Paul Cahill and Billy by Gary Brown. While the other two spend their time being a nuisance, Billy wants to work on a farm. He sees it as an opportunity of doing a job he'd really enjoy, of fulfilling a dream and making a fresh start. The conflict and violence in the play arose out of a clash between the quick Liverpool talk of the three lads and the slower Lancashire talk of the farm hands. In an interview with Benedict Nightingale entitled 'Willy and the Poor Boys' published in Radio Times (23.1.1975) p.15-17, Willy Russell talked about 'The Death of a Young, Young Man', and said it was about prejudice and being trapped by circumstances. He also said that all his plays have a 'strong narrative content and generally make direct contact with the audience'. The play starts with a monologue directed straight at the viewer in his living room by Bo. The director of the play was Viktors Ritelis who said it was the most exciting thing he'd worked on during the past ten years. The violent death at the end is reminiscent of 'Blood Brothers', but the central situation in the play of a worthwhile individual trying to escape difficult circumstances was a theme that has emerged again and again in Russell's work for stage and television.

'Breezeblock Park' (1975)

'Breezeblock Park' was first performed at the Everyman Theatre, Liverpool on 8th May 1975 and opened at the Mermaid Theatre, London on 12th September 1977, before transferring to the Whitehall Theatre on 3rd November 1977. It was described by Russell as a 'Liverpool comedy of (bad) manners' or 'Liverpool behind the curtains'. It is an imaginative reworking of his own family life. He decided to write it after seeing Alan Ayckbourn's trilogy 'The Norman Conquests' at the Globe when his own 'John, Paul, George, Ringo ... and Bert' was at the Lyric in the West End in 1974. In his play, Ayckbourn exposed the way of life of a middle class family on stage and the middle class audience loved seeing itself. In Ayckbourn's 'Table Manners', Annie tries to break away from her dull life looking after her invalid mother to have a 'dirty weekend' with Norman at East Grinstead. The family prevent her from going away, in a similar way as Sandra's family in 'Breezeblock Park' try and stop her breaking away from the family clan. Russell suddenly realized that he wanted to write a play about Liverpool working class family life. It was a brave decision as lesser artists would have been tempted to follow the success of The Beatles musical with another 'pop' musical. Russell liked the drawing room scene and the satisfying unity of the traditional English comedy of manners as written by Wilde, Coward and Rattigan. It is a very entertaining and thought-provoking play which is so funny that you can miss the underlying seriousness. Like most of his plays, it depends on his brilliant handling of Liverpool dialect and a strong story line. It was originally called 'Reservations' because of the reference to the working class being herded together in council housing estates like Indians on a reservation, with the extra sense of the author having 'reservations' about the situation. But Russell dropped this title on the advice of Alan Dossor, who pointed out that the critics could have a field day with such a title. 'Breezeblock Park' has also been referred to as 'Bleasdale Park' occasionally!

'One for the Road' (1976-79)

Russell's plays need updating because their realism requires topical reference, particularly for the humour, and none more so than his much rewritten and re-named play 'One For the Road': 'I've been re-writing it for eleven years' he said in 1987. The play was commissioned by Contact Theatre in Manchester with funds donated by the North West Arts Association. The original title was to be 'Tupperware Man' but because of legal difficulties the show was called 'Painted Veg and Parkinson'! The

Willy Russell outside the Liverpool Playhouse for the July 1980 production of 'One For The Road'.

firm of Tupperware did not press for any changes in the script as long as Russell changed the title. 'Painted Veg and Parkinson' (the worst title of any of Russell's plays) played to fifty one per cent of capacity for fourteen performances at Contact Theatre in Manchester in November and December 1976. The play was re-named 'Dennis The Menace' which was altered to 'One For the Road' because when 'Dennis The Menace' played at Norwich, the theatre was full of children, expecting to see The Beano's famous character! It had also been called 'Happy Returns'. Russell's wife

82

Annie suggested the title of 'One For the Road' shortly before it opened at Nottingham Playhouse in March 1979, directed by Mike Ockrent. Just as 'Breezeblock Park' counterpointed Christmas with family crisis, so 'One For the Road' counterpoints a dinner party with disaster in the form of the host's manic behaviour - what a way to treat his guests! Russell used the same sort of contrast in 'Stags and Hens', counterpointing the wedding romance that we might expect with a bleakly realistic look at a doomed relationship in a broken-down club in a dying city.

'Break in' (1977)

Willy Russell's T.V. play 'Break In', a BBC2 play in the series 'Scene: New Plays For Young People', was screened on 14th August 1977. It was not given the usual repeat on Schools T.V. (for which it was originally made) because teachers thought it might encourage kids to vandalise their schools. There was a feeling that even with a teacher to discuss the play - the principle on which all schools programmes are designed - the seeds of provocation might be sown. 'Break In' is written in Liverpool dialect and the drama unfolds using flashbacks with twenty five short scenes. The play opens in a Probation Officer's room. Macka, played by Peter Riley, is being questioned about a break in at his school. Macka and two of his mates, Yosser and Snowy broke in to retrieve a football which, ironically, they'd stolen in the first place and which had been confiscated by an unsympathetic caretaker called Dixie. Macka ends up smashing the school after reading an unfavourable note to the Royal Navy and realizing that this will ruin his dreams of a career in the navy. The play confronts the waste of a no-hoper like Macka.

'Our Day Out' (1977)

When Willy Russell taught at Shorefields Comprehensive School in 1973 and 1974, he worked in the remedial department with a woman called Dorothy King whose approach reminded Russell of A.S.Neill of Summerhill School. She mothered the remedial, but streetwise kids, and every year she took a group of them for a day out to Conway in North Wales. She used to prepare a booklet and the kids were supposed to gather information on the trip, but her main idea was to give them a good day out. Willy Russell went on the 1974 trip and, right at the last minute, a Deputy Head joined the group. He was an old-fashioned, authoritarian type of man, but he became humanised by the children. This stiff teacher was charmed by the kids into relaxing and enjoying a great day and forgetting his chosen role as an authority figure. He blossomed as a human being and the kids loved him, but when the coach returned to Liverpool and he was getting off he turned and suddenly shouted at a girl because she'd not come in school uniform. In that moment he undid all the good work he'd done throughout the day. Russell remembers seeing that episode clearly and thinking it was the absolute genesis of a drama: a complete reversal in a human being. It is about the only play he's ever written where he can say 'Yes, consciously I saw on this day the framework for what later became "Our Day Out".' It was eighteen months after leaving the school that he found a way, in 1975, to write the film based upon the day's

83

events. None of the material in the film happened in the way he finally wrote it, none of the words used in the film were actually said in that way. 'Our Day Out' takes the spirit of the day. Russell himself went on a trip to the Blue John Mines in Derbyshire as a child and remembers kids getting up to all kinds of antics. He sees the school trip as a modern legend and wanted the film to reflect a sense of legend. When teachers discuss such trips, invariably one of them tells of a child who got lost. Of course, Carol doesn't get lost, she chooses to stay behind.

Russell found 'Our Day Out' very easy to write and it took only five days in its original long-hand form, maybe because it was based on reality. When the film was typed out, Russell sent it to David Rose, who was then Head of BBC Drama and has until recently been in charge of Channel 4's 'Film on Four'. Rose had overseen the production of an earlier Russell play for the BBC ('King of the Castle') and Russell expected him to be delighted with it. But Rose saw how expensive the film would be to make and wrote to Russell's agent Margaret Ramsay saying that the BBC could not afford to make it that year. Then the script was sent to Granada TV but while they had it Rose admitted he'd made a big mistake and agreed to do the film. Russell later learnt that Rose's script editor Pedr James, the eventual director of 'Our Day Out' persuaded Rose to take a closer look at the script and forget the budget. Subsequently, 'Our Day Out' has been sold to T.V. stations all over the world.

Russell was very much involved in the pre-production stage of the film, helping the director to make decisions about casting and locations and making script alterations. The script went through several drafts before it was ready for filming. There was a fundamental re-write of the scene on the roadside cafe where the kids plunder the stock as the director was worried about the morality of it. There was no justification for the looting of sweets by the kids. In looking at the first draft Russell felt the scene did not fit in with the rest of the piece. The cafe was run by two Scotsmen who were rather caricatured, so he changed the ownership to Welsh women who exploited the kids. However, he still feels it did not make it morally justifiable because two wrongs don't add up to a right. It seemed to satisfy the director and producer, who feared floods of letters accusing the BBC of encouraging robbery, in which case their defence was that the proprietors were ready to rob the kids so there was a rough sort of justice.

Russell went on location in Liverpool, but his only involvement was to point out to the director and cameraman that they had not picked up a crucial shot during the opening sequence when Les the Lollipop Man stops Mr. Briggs' car. When it was brought to the attention of the director it was agreed to return to Liverpool to shoot the missing scene. Russell was heavily involved during the editing process, watching about eight hours of the film footage which was reduced in the first rough cut to ninety minutes. After viewing, it was cut by fifteen minutes. There was a scene in the script when Carol is on the cliff and all her teachers are looking for her. An old Welshman approaches Carol and sees that she is out of her environment. There was some nice dialogue in which she said she was a doctor's daughter who lived in a white house. This scene had to go because it duplicated the scene with Briggs where she says she wants to stay and live there.

The children in the film were chosen mainly by the director Pedr James. Willy and Annie Russell selected about five Liverpool schools with sympathetic headmasters and English teachers, including Dingle Vale where Willy had taught. Pedr James spent a week going to each of these schools. He sat in on lessons and selected faces he thought would fit. He then heard this group read. Those unable to read well were not chosen or offered a non-speaking part. There was one kid who insisted on being auditioned but at that time was largely unable to read. Because he'd been so insistent and wanted to be a star and looked right he was given a non-speaking part, then he took over another kid's speaking role whose parents had objected to their child being portrayed as a scallywag. The selection was based on whether the child looked right and could perform the script.

'Our Day Out' was written as a T.V. play, then adapted as a stage musical. Only the camera could capture the performance and waif-like appearance of Julie Jones as Carol, and the passing scenery, but despite its limitations the stage musical works well.

'Our Day Out' (Musical, 1983)

A musical version of 'Our Day Out' had already been in Russell's mind before Bob Eaton, the then Director of the Everyman Theatre in Liverpool, asked Russell if he would turn the T.V. play into a stage musical. Russell then became heavily involved with 'Blood Brothers', which took longer than he had envisaged. He had committed himself to doing 'Our Day Out' for the Everyman as a joint production with their Youth Theatre. He somewhat reluctantly allowed the Everyman to workshop the piece on the basis that he would sit down with Bob Eaton and quickly decide where songs would go, which songs would be used and which songs Willy himself would write. Bob Eaton and Chris Mellors (the Youth Theatre Musical Director) were to write the rest of the songs with collaboration from Willy. This arrangement actually worked very well.

With the Everyman Youth Theatre, Russell stuck to the script and didn't let them improvise because he believes that if you allow children complete licence to improvise, a lot of good ideas are frittered away. But the kids in this very vital Youth Theatre responded with excellent performances. To include all thirty of the group two companies were used, who alternated their performances in the theatre with the six professional actors. 'Our Day Out' was first performed at the Everyman from 8th April to 7th May 1983.

'I Read the News Today' (1977)

Russell's wryly amusing radio play 'I Read the News Today' was commissioned and first broadcast on 4th February 1977 by the BBC in a schools radio series called 'Listening and Writing'. In the play, Paul Ross is a trendy D.J. broadcasting at night

85

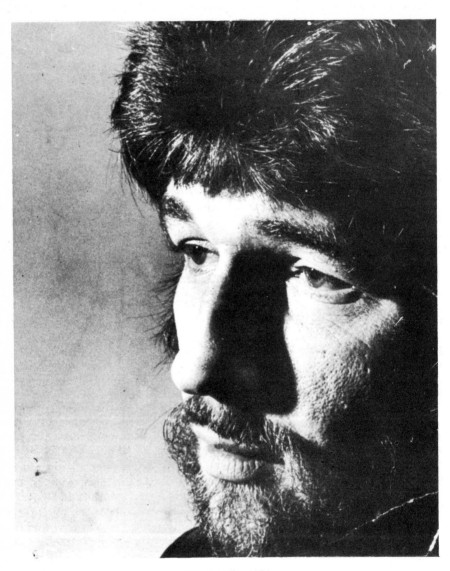

Willy Russell in 1976

in a radio station 'anywhere'. An advert for 'Soundpack' is played, which claims that it enables you to produce wonderful music. Ross reads the news which concerns a youth called Ronald Arthur Heron who has escaped from the police after being sentenced for causing over five thousand pounds' worth of damage to 'Soundpacks' in a local warehouse. The sound of a scuffle is heard and Heron bursts in with a gun and ties Ross up. The play ends with The Beatles' song 'A Day in the Life'. 'I Read the News Today' is a skilfully written radio play about a drama in a radio studio. We do not realise until the end that Heron was not telling the truth about the gun, as the story he told to Ross seemed convincing and his criticism of 'junk culture' had a ring of truth. 'I Read the News Today' is the only radio play Russell has written and it displays his versatility in adapting to another medium while again demonstrating his mastery of plot, dialogue and character.

'Lies' (1978)

In his T.V. play 'Lies' Parts I and II, Russell writes about lies, false impressions and self-deceptions, themes he had touched on in 'I read the news today'. 'Lies' are short plays first broadcast in two parts by BBC Schools Television in the series 'Scene', so they were written with a teenage audience of school children in mind. The plays were first broadcast in November 1978, were repeated in October 1983, and concern Sammy Stubbs, who was played by Stephen McManaman.

'Lies' Part I begins with Sammy, a fifteen year-old schoolboy from a one parent family in inner city Liverpool, playing truant from school in the city centre with his friend Rolo. Sammy has a worthy (if far-fetched) dream of escaping with his mother and brother Terry to Cornwall, of buying a derelict house and doing it up. Rolo is, by contrast, a cynical, narrow-minded thief. Sammy is a well-meaning lad, despite playing truant from school. He is gullible but enterprising in a humble way and is always on the look-out for opportunities to make some legitimate money by collecting the supermarket trolleys or helping move boxes in the big stores. Rolo thinks Sammy is a 'nutter' for having this kind of attitude. Sammy is rather like Billy in 'The Death of a Young, Young Man', while Rolo is like Cazza or Bo. Sammy's house is very dingy and his mother is not well. Mrs. Stubbs is on tablets and says 'I'm thirty-five an' I feel more like sixty-five' which almost echoes Mrs. Johnstone's line in 'Blood Brothers' when she sings 'By the time I was twenty-five I looked like forty-two' in the song 'Marilyn Monroe'. Mrs. Stubbs is another of Russell's characters who feel old before their time. She blames 'this place' - her home in Liverpool : 'Livin' in this place ages y' before y' time'. She reminisces about her 'hey-day' when she was twenty and, again like Mrs. Johnstone, used to go dancing. Another likeness between Mrs. Stubbs and Mrs. Johnston is that they've both been left by their respective husbands. Mrs. Stubbs complains that as soon as a man has had a woman, he doesn't treat her as well as he did before, and Shirley Valentine was to feel the same about men.

'Stags and Hens' (1978)

'Stags and Hens' was first written as part of an exercise for students of television at Manchester Polytechnic where Russell had a Fellowship in Creative Writing from 1977 to 1979. The first version was performed by students on closed circuit T.V. Artistic Director Chris Bond encouraged Willy to turn this 'in house' T.V. piece into a stage play for the Liverpool Everyman. Running for eight weeks from October 11th 1978, it was a huge hit, but it wasn't taken up immediately by any other theatre. Not until 1982 was it revived, by the Duke's Playhouse, Lancaster. It was then repeated at Liverpool Playhouse, and played in London at the Young Vic in 1987. 'Stags and Hens' is a brutally realistic comedy about the rival claims of tribal behaviour and individuality in Liverpool. The play is completely unsentimental about Liverpool, seeing it as a dying city which traps the people who live there. The scene is set in the Ladies and Gents at a Liverpool dance hall one evening on the eve of Linda's and Dave's marriage. Russell said of the setting : 'That's where all the real action is on these occasions - the girls spend the evening making up, and the lads spend it throwing up'. Apart from a mortuary, you could not get further away from wedding romance than the loos in a tough Liverpool club! The drama unfolds out of a fortuitous coincidence as both stags and hens arrive at the same club, a device akin to the use of double booking which Alan Bleasdale used in his film 'No Surrender'.

Russell said that 'Stags and Hens' is a development of his obsession with people trying to break away from tribal living. It is a play with rough humour, strong language and insight into the tribalism of Liverpool life and the ties of loyalty. It makes no concessions whatsoever to sensitive preconceptions about language and drama. Russell also wrote the screenplay of 'Stags and Hens' called 'Dancin' thru the Dark' which was filmed in Liverpool. Released in 1990, it starred Con O'Neill and was co-produced by Russell's wife Annie, together with Andree Molyneux who produced 'Break In' and 'Lies' for the B.B.C.

'Daughters of Albion' (1979)

In 'Stags and Hens' Linda escaped but in 'Daughters of Albion', Russell's T.V. play, three biscuit factory workers who have the opportunity of breaking away cannot bring themselves to do so. 'Daughters of Albion' is an hour-long play broadcast on 1st May 1979 on ITV as part of the 'ITV Playhouse' series. The play was commissioned by Yorkshire T.V. who then surprisingly rejected it, so it was sent to the BBC. Meanwhile, David Cunliffe, who was shortly to start work at Yorkshire, had read the script and decided it had to be produced. It was directed by Pedr James who had previously directed Russell's 'Our Day Out' for the BBC with such distinction, and who took over as Artistic Director of the Liverpool Everyman in May 1979. The literary origin of the play's title derives from William Blake's poem 'Visions of the Daughters of Albion' written in 1794. Albion is a common poetical name for England. Albion's daughters are Englishwomen, enslaved in the social mores of their time, who weep over their sorrows and long for freedom. Russell also knew the Liverpool poet

88

'The Gang of Four' Artistic Directors of the Liverpool Playhouse, 1981: Bill Morrison, Alan Bleasdale, Willy Russell and Chris Bond. (Solo Syndication)

Adrian Henri's poem 'Mrs. Albion You've Got A Lovely Daughter' published in The Mersey Sound, Penguin Modern Poets volume of 1967. This poem concerns the sexual adventures of young Liverpool girls. In Russell's play, two of the three girls have sexual experiences (and the third wants to) but this is set in a wider social context. One source for the play was Russell's memory of going to an all-night party at a large mock-Georgian house in West Derby, Liverpool as a fifteen year-old. But, as in all his work, he transforms his own experience in the white heat of his imagination. The play's executive producer, David Cunliffe, was right in saying that it was both a social comment and a lot of fun. Pedr James scoured Liverpool seeking the right girls to cast for the three biscuit factory workers who accidentally go to the wrong all-night party, one for university graduates after their final exams. After auditioning about three hundred girls he chose three - Annette Ekblom who plays Kathleen, Kate Fitzgerald who plays Sharon and Janet Rawson who plays Tracey. The language is realistic and the plot is cleverly devised to bring the working-class girls into contact with the middle-class students.

'The Boy with the Transistor Radio' (1980)

'The Boy with the Transistor Radio' is a thirty minute T.V. play which was written

89

Willy Russell co-directing 'Educating Rita' at Liverpool Playhouse in January 1981 with Pip Broughton (2nd right), Kate Fitzgerald and William Gaunt.

for a Thames T.V. series for schools called 'The English Programme' and broadcast on 26th February 1980 and 21st January 1981. It is about Terry Davies, a teenager living in an inner-city area of Liverpool, who listens to the radio all the time and is about to leave school. It is a reworked and much improved version of Russell's earlier play 'Keep Your Eyes Down'. It could be retitled 'Low Expectations' : Terry's expectations are great but no-one shares them. There are several autobiographical elements in the play. Terry (played by Simon Driver) is in the bottom set in a comprehensive school, he likes the guitar and music, and he goes to work in a warehouse. Most of all, like Willy Russell as a teenager, Terry feels trapped by circumstances and low expectations.

The play starts with Bill Withers singing 'Lovely Day' in the background with views of some very unlovely Liverpool environment: people going to work on a grey, cold morning, waiting at bus stops or coming off the ferry at the Pier Head. Throughout the play, reality is counterpointed with Terry's fantasy world until the very end when he discovers the fantasy to be worthless and turns towards a reality of his own.

'Politics and Terror' (1980)

'Politics and Terror' is an eight minute, one-act play written for children. It was

90

Willy Russell inside the Odeon, Liverpool to celebrate forty weeks of 'Educating Rita'.

commissioned by Granada T.V. and broadcast on 28th February 1980 in the programme 'Celebration'. There are only three characters - George, Chris and Tommo. Chris has been to the supermarket and bought sweets. George wants a sweet but Chris won't give him one. So George uses lies and fear (the politics and terror of the title) to trick Chris into handing over his sweets. This is a funny short play, written in scouse dialect, and resembles part of a scene in Act I of 'Blood Brothers' when Edward comes to Mickey's street with sweets. In the T.V. play, Chris Darwin played Chris, George Costigan played George and Tommo was played by Julia North. 'Politics and Terror' has been produced on the professional stage by the Coliseum Theatre Company, Oldham in summer 1982 as part of a comical collection of songs and sketches from leading northern writers called 'A Little Of What You Fancy'.

<u>'Educating Rita'</u> (1980)

The R.S.C.'s Literary Manager, Walter Donohue, had been impressed by 'Breezeblock Park' during its run at The Mermaid Theatre, London in 1977. He commissioned Willy Russell to write, for £700, a play for The Warehouse (Donmar Theatre) in London, a small theatre with a capacity of two hundred. 'Educating Rita' was originally booked to play twenty-one performances only in this Covent Garden

91

Willy Russell outside the Odeon, Liverpool, 24 March 1983.

theatre, such was the lack of faith by the R.S.C. Trevor Nunn saved it for the R.S.C after they'd sent it to the Royal Court. In the first draft of 'Educating Rita' Frank hardly existed, Russell had virtually written a one-hander. In the new draft, he developed the relationship between Frank and Rita. 'Educating Rita' opened at The Warehouse with Julie Walters and Mark Kingston on 10th June 1980, then transferred with the same cast to the Piccadilly Theatre on 19th August 1980. It became the longest-running play at the Piccadilly for twenty years, running for over two years with more than eight hundred performances. Over forty thousand people saw the Liverpool Playhouse production in 1981 which Russell co-directed with Pip Broughton. There was a United Kingdom tour from the 30th August 1982 to the 12th March 1983. Tom Baker and Kate Fitzgerald played in this up to and including the 18th December and Ken Farrington took over the rest of the tour, beginning from the 3rd January, while Kate Fitzgerald remained as Rita throughout.

The title was originally a working title which Russell decided to keep. It is taken from the 'Educating Archie' radio show with Peter Brough where the ventriloquist is outsmarted by his dummy, a strange situation for a radio show! The play has

*'Blood Brothers': Wendy Murray (Mrs Lyons), Willy Russell and Barbara Dickson (Mrs Johnstone) at
the Liverpool Playhouse, 6 January 1983.*

similarities with Shaw's 'Pygmalion', Williams' 'The Corn is Green' and Wesker's 'Roots' in terms of the relationship between class and education, but 'Educating Rita' comes from Russell's own imaginative reworking of experience and is very autobiographical. He wrote the play in twelve weeks, partly in the back room of his in-laws' home in Staplands Road, Liverpool. This room is the model for the set of the play: it's a study with books on shelves all round the room from floor to ceiling and a desk with typewriter and chair.

'Educating Rita' (Screenplay, 1983)

Willy Russell wrote the screenplay for the film of 'Educating Rita' which was originally commissioned by Columbia. When they held the rights, they wanted to cast Dolly Parton as Rita and Paul Newman as Frank. Dolly Parton sent the script back and said she'd read it when it was translated into American! They wanted to change the play into one about a black woman and devise a way of getting Rita into bed with Frank, but these ideas were not acceptable to Willy Russell. The director of the film was Lewis Gilbert, whose credits go back to 'Reach for the Sky'. The film, starring Julie Walters and Michael Caine, won three Academy Award nominations and also won three Golden Globe awards in 1984. It cost 4 million dollars to make, but earned 14 million dollars. Willy Russell was nominated as best screenwriter for the American Academy Awards (Oscars).

Russell said that the screenplay 'felt like a new piece of work'. The screenplay involved writing dialogue for twenty new characters mentioned in the stage play such as Denny, Trish, Rita's father, Frank's girlfriend Julia and Frank's academic colleagues and Russell spent five weeks in Cannes writing it. A considerable amount of Rita's criticism of her working-class background in Act I is omitted in the film and there is greater emphasis on the relationship between Frank and Rita as people and not so much as tutor and student.

'Blood Brothers' (1983)

Russell had first thought up the idea for 'Blood Brothers' in 1976 and at one stage considered writing it for his R.S.C. commission but changed his mind. His play, as distinct from the musical, about twins parted at birth and brought up in different environments was commissioned by Paul Harman, director of Merseyside Young People's Theatre Company. Russell wrote it in five weeks, with one song, 'Marilyn Monroe'. It also became a part of a BBC schools programme about Russell as a writer. The first performance was on 9th November 1981 at Fazakerley Comprehensive School in Liverpool. There were sixty performances of the play in local schools. The original production was designed for an audience of 120 at most, to be played on the floor of a school hall with chairs arranged on four sides of a square with room for access at each corner. The scene changes and the interventions by the narrator were marked by freezes and the sound of wooden sticks being knocked together. The play lasted seventy minutes and it was performed by five actors with no sets and one unaccompanied song. This small-scale production was a great success.

The full-scale musical 'Blood Brothers' for which Russell wrote the music, lyrics and book, had its world premiere at the Liverpool Playhouse on 8th January 1983 and subsequently transferred to the Lyric Theatre in Shaftesbury Avenue. It is currently in the fifth year of its second London run. It won four prestigious awards including one for Barbara Dickson, and has been very widely performed. Russell had been working on transforming the play into a musical throughout 1982. During that period (1981-1983) he was a reluctant Associate Director at Liverpool Playhouse together with Alan Bleasdale, Chris Bond and Bill Morrison. In terms of style 'Blood Brothers'

Willy Russell on stage as the narrator-milkman in 'Blood Brothers' at the Empire Theatre, Liverpool, August 1984. (Phil Cutts)

is related to Russell's earlier Everyman work 'When the Reds', 'Sam O'Shanker' and 'John, Paul, George, Ringo ... and Bert', with the interweaving of realistic dialogue, songs integrated into the action, and a rapid succession of scenes spanning a long time. Russell wanted 'Blood Brothers' to be seen as an English musical presented through Merseyside. It is very Liverpudlian with unemployment, superstition, crime, poverty, sex, violence, humour and class conflict reflecting the sometimes harsh social experience of Liverpool people.

Willy Russell and the original Shirley Valentine, April 1986.

Pauline Collins as Shirley, Vaudeville Theatre, London, January 1988. (Catherine Ashmore)

'One Summer' (1984)

Willy Russell had a major disagreement with Yorkshire Television over the casting of his five-part series of T.V. plays 'One Summer', first shown in 1984. Russell wanted younger boys to play the parts of the two Liverpool lads Billy and Icky. Russell insisted they left his name off the credits as a result of this argument. Russell claimed that Yorkshire TV, who made the film for Channel 4, had reneged on an agreement that they would take his name off the series if he was dissatisfied. Russell disowned the series, but Channel 4 advertised it as being by the author of 'Educating Rita'. Russell also disliked the way the company had changed the bias of the story during production.

'Shirley Valentine' (1986)

Obviously, one of the strengths of Willy Russell as a writer is his ability to express the female point of view. He writes roles for women that one could believe were actually written by a woman. Margaret Kitchen of the Liverpool Daily Post noticed this quality in a performance reading by Willy Russell of 'Shirley Valentine' at the Liverpool Everyman in March 1986. Russell had taken over the role at short notice when the star of this one-woman show, Noreen Kershaw, was struck down with appendicitis. Margaret Kitchen wrote that 'Willy Russell's "Shirley Valentine" has much to say about being a woman and is remarkable for being written so sensitively by a man. The playwright's own reading of the work is so sensitive that it is possible to entirely forget a man is speaking the words ... the reading is not only a rare theatrical event, it is a rare moment of communication between the sexes'.

Russell likes to ring the changes in terms of form, so after 'Blood Brothers' we could expect something different, and 'Shirley Valentine' is an audacious departure in form. However, one practical reason for writing a one-woman play was a tight schedule. Glen Walford, the Artistic Director of the Everyman Theatre, had commissioned Russell to write a play or preferably a musical to mark the Everyman's 21st anniversary in the spring of 1986. The posters advertising the 'new Willy Russell show' were already on display in Liverpool when he returned from holiday in France with no idea of what he was going to write.

'Shirley Valentine' is a two hour long monologue spoken by Shirley. Russell had seen Billy Connolly's stage act on T.V. and thought it might be possible to extend that kind of stand-up comedian's routine as a play. He had originally seen Connolly's 'Big Welly Boot Show' at the Edinburgh Festival of 1972 and also knew him from the folk club circuit. For the name, Shirley Valentine, Russell remembered a girl at Rainford High School. She apparently is not at all like Russell's character, and was amazed when she saw posters around Liverpool with her name on them.

Despite being a one-woman play, there's no shortage of characters. Shirley herself is a vulnerable and loveable person and engages our sympathy and imagination as she talks about her husband Joe, her children Brian and Millandra, her next door neighbour Gillian, her old class mate Marjorie Majors, her feminist friend Jane and her Greek lover Costas. These people are brought vividly to life in Russell's brilliant writing. The play is a portrait of an ordinary woman's struggle to regenerate her life and the Greek island setting of Act II has more than literal significance. Greece, the birthplace of Western civilisation, is the perfect symbolic setting for the birth of Shirley's new life. The play deals in emotions but this is a strength, not a weakness. Shirley opens her heart to us and the audience relate to her as an insecure human being. The drama and comedy arise out of her struggle to make her mind up to go to Greece, then actually to carry the idea through. Her role as a working class scouse mother and wife conceals a frustrated person longing for a new life worth living. Shirley has lost the youthful love of life she had when as Shirley Valentine she fell in love with 'a boy called Joe'. As 'auto-mother' to Brian and Millandra, she functions only to serve the needs of others. She has sacrificed herself in marriage to a narrow-minded husband and become 'St Joan of the Fitted Units'. For those who know Brecht's 'St Joan of the Stockyards' there is an added layer but the line also strikes a chord with those who have never heard of Brecht. Shirley is a woman trapped in imprisoning circumstances, seeking escape to a personally fulfilling life. She is in some ways like an older version of Linda in 'Blood Brothers': although their circumstances differ, they both dream, as the Narrator says of Linda in Act II: 'There's a girl inside the woman/Who's waiting to get free/She's washed a million dishes/She's always making tea'.

Willy Russell was presented with the Comedy of the Year Award for 'Shirley Valentine' at the Laurence Olivier Awards in January 1989. Pauline Collins was named Actress of the Year for her role as Shirley. 'Shirley Valentine' opened at New York's Booth Theatre on 16th February 1989, again with Pauline Collins as Shirley, to great critical and popular acclaim. The film of 'Shirley Valentine' directed by Lewis Gilbert was released in Britain in Autumn 1989 with Pauline Collins as Shirley and Tom Conti as Costas, with roles for Joanna Lumley and Julie McKenzie, and cameo roles for Russell's two young daughters (Ruth and Rachel).

'Terraces' (1993)

'Terraces' was originally written about 1973 but it was not made for T.V. as the cost of painting and re-painting a street was too great for the slender budget of B.B.C. Schools' Drama for which it was intended. The new version of 'Terraces' will be screened in January 1993 by the B.B.C, starring Mark Womack. The first version was concisely written with seventeen short scenes. The title refers to a terrace of houses and to terraces at a football ground and the play concerns Danny Harris's refusal to conform to the attitudes of all the other people in his street who want to show their support for a football team by painting their houses the team's colour - yellow. There is a tremendous conflict in the play between peer-group pressure to conform, and Danny Harris's sense of his own individuality. The tension between tribal allegiance and individualism is central to many of Russell's plays especially 'Breezeblock Park', 'Stags and Hens' and 'Educating Rita' and was strongly present in his very first play 'Keep Your Eyes Down'.

BIBLIOGRAPHY

1. Primary Sources: Playscripts

'Keep Your Eyes Down' (1971), Unity Theatre Archive, Merseyside Museum of Labour History, Liverpool.

'Sam O'Shanker' (1973), British Theatre Association Play Library, London.

'John, Paul, George, Ringo... and Bert' (1974), British Theatre Association Play Library, London.

'Playground' (1972), 'When The Reds' (1973), 'The Cantril Tales' (1974), Willy Russell's Collection.

2. Published Plays

Willy Russell, 'Terraces', Terraces, ed. Alan Durband, Hutchinson, London 1973.

Willy Russell, Breezeblock Park, Samuel French, London 1978.

Willy Russell, 'I Read The News Today', Home Truths, Three Plays, Longman, Harlow, 1982.

Willy Russell, 'I Read The News Today' Responses. The Wild Bunch and other Plays, ed. Don Shiach, Thomas Nelson, Walton-on-Thames 1990.

Willy Russell, I Read the News Today, Samuel French, London, 1987.

Willy Russell, 'Break In', Scene Scripts Two, Longman Imprint Books, ed. Michael Marland, London 1978.

Willy Russell, One For The Road, Samuel French, London 1980, rev. and rewritten, Samuel French, London 1985.

Willy Russell, 'Our Day Out', Act One, ed. David Self and Ray Speakman, Hutchinson, London 1979.

Willy Russell, Our Day Out, A Play by Willy Russell with songs and music by Bob Eaton, Chris Mellors and Willy Russell, Methuen, London 1984.

Willy Russell, Our Day Out, A Play with music, songs and music by Bob Eaton, Chris Mellorsand Willy Russell, Samuel French, London 1984.

Willy Russell, Our Day Out and Other Plays, Studio Scripts, ed. David Self,

Hutchinson, London 1987.

Willy Russell, 'Lies' Parts I & II, City Life, Studio Scripts, ed. David Self, Hutchinson, London 1980.

Willy Russell, Stags and Hens, Samuel French, London 1985.

Willy Russell, 'Daughters of Albion', Willy Russell and Polly Teale, Opportunity Knocks? Two Plays about life after school, ed. Ray Speakman, Heinemann 1986.

Willy Russell, 'The Boy with the Transistor Radio', Working, Studio Scripts, ed. David Self, Hutchinson, London 1980.

Willy Russell, 'Politics and Terror', Wordplays I, ed. Alan Durband, Hutchinson, London 1982.

Willy Russell, Educating Rita, Samuel French, London 1981.

Willy Russell, Educating Rita, Longman Study Text, ed. Richard Adams, Harlow 1985.

Willy Russell, Educating Rita, Stags and Hens and Blood Brothers, Two Plays and a Musical, Methuen, London 1986.

Willy Russell, Blood Brothers, Samuel French, London 1985.

Willy Russell, Blood Brothers, Introduction and notes by Chas White and Chris Shepherd, Hutchinson, London 1986.

Willy Russell, Shirley Valentine and One For The Road, Methuen, London 1988.

Willy Russell, Shirley Valentine, Samuel French, London 1988.

3. Selected Secondary Material

The Everyman Theatre, Liverpool

Michael Coveney, 'Working the System', Plays and Players, December 1973, p.16-19.
Michael Coveney, 'Everyman in Good Humour', Plays and Players, August 1975, p.12-15.
Doreen Tanner, Everyman: the first ten years, Liverpool 1975.
Nick Shrimpton, 'Everyman in Good Humour', Plays and Players, December 1977, p.35.

Bob Eaton, 'Everyman Theatre, Liverpool', Drama, Autumn 1982.

John McGrath

John McGrath, A Good Night Out. Popular Theatre: Audience, Class and Form,
 Methuen, London 1981.
Oscar Moore, 'Behind the Fringe', Plays and Players, April 1983, p.11-13.

McGrath's 'Unruly Elements'

Eric Shorter, 'Play's satire too rambling to succeed', Daily Telegraph, 11 March,
 1971.
Irving Wardle, 'Unruly Elements', The Times, 11 March, 1971.

Willy Russell's 'Keep Your Eyes Down' (1971)

Anon, 'Pleasant shock for drama audience', Liverpool Weekly News, 16 December, 1971.
Anon, 'Willie makes his debut as a playwright', Liverpool Echo, 9 December,
 1971, p.5.

'Blind Scouse' 1972

Doreen Tanner, 'Mersey Mixture: a trio for the festival fringe', Liverpool Daily
 Post, 29 June, 1972.

'When The Reds' 1973

Charles Lewsen, 'Football saga', The Times, 30 March, 1973.
H.R., 'Now the Kop humour goes on stage', Liverpool Echo, 29 March, 1973.
Robin Thornber, 'When The Reds... in Liverpool', The Guardian, 29 March,
 1973.

'John, Paul, George, Ringo ... and Bert' 1974

John Barber, 'Musical tells Beatles story with bite', Daily Telegraph, 16 August,
 1974.
Michael Coveney, 'John, Paul, George, Ringo ... and Bert', The Financial Times,
 24 May, 1974.
Adrian Henri, 'John, Paul, George, Ringo and Bert', Plays and Players, Septem-
 ber 1974, p.36-7.
Dusty Hughes, 'Band on the Run', Time Out, August 2-8, 1974, p.14-15.
J. W. Lambert, 'London Theatre: The beat and the beaten', The Sunday Times, 18
 August, 1974, p.31.
Angela Neustatter, 'Interview with Willy Russell', The Guardian, 14 August,
 1974, p.10.

Hughie Ross, 'Beatlemania is revived again', Liverpool Echo, 22 May, 1974, p.13.
Sue Sellers, 'It's Yesterday Once More', Liverpool Daily Post, 12 August, 1974, p.6.
Don Smith, 'Everyman's Beatles', Liverpool Daily Post, 8 May, 1974, p.6.
Don Smith, 'The World of Willy Russell Takes Off', Liverpool Daily Post, 28 June, 1974, p.6.
Robin Thornber, 'John, Paul, George, Ringo ... and Bert', The Guardian, 22 May, 1974, p.12.
Irving Wardle, 'John, Paul, George, Ringo ... and Bert', The Times, 16 August, 1974, p.12.

'The Cantril Tales' 1974

Philip Key, 'Makings of a very funny show', Liverpool Daily Post, 27 December, 1974, p.3.
Gillian Linscott, '"The Cantril Tales" at Liverpool Everyman', The Guardian, 28 December, 1974.
M.B.M., 'Liverpool. "The Cantril Tales"', The Stage, 9 January 1975.
Joe Riley, 'Cantril Tales a great success', Liverpool Echo, 30 December, 1974, p.9.

'The Death of a Young, Young Man' 1975

Nancy Banks-Smith, 'Television', The Guardian, 31 January, 1975.
Mary Malone, 'The wild country', Daily Mirror, 31 January, 1975.
Benedict Nightingale, 'Willy and the Poor Boys', Radio Times, 23 January, 1975, p.15-17
Spencer Leigh, 'Rise of a Young, Young Man', Lancashire Life, August, 1974, p.57.
Joe Riley, 'Plays by City Writers to appear on TV', Liverpool Echo, 6 January, 1975, p.8.

'Breezeblock Park' 1975

W. Stephen Gilbert, 'Breezeblock Park', Plays and Players, November 1977, p.27.
Philip Key, 'Well-worn path but still a funny one', Liverpool Daily Post, 9 May 1975. p.5.
Bernard Levin, 'Gilbert Pinfold sees it through', The Sunday Times, 18 September, 1977, p.35.
Joe Riley, 'Why Willy won't disown his past', Liverpool Echo, 7 May, 1975, p.6.
Joe Riley, 'Party Fun in Breezeblock Park', Liverpool Echo, 9 May, 1975, p.3.

'Break In' 1977

Peter Fiddick, 'Out of their class', The Guardian, 2 August, 1977.

'One For The Road' 1976-79

Michael Billington, 'Getting the Abbot Habit', The Guardian, 23 October, 1987, p.20.
Peter Hepple, 'Dennis the Menace', The Stage, 29 October, 1987, p.13.
Philip Key, 'It's Russell to the rescue', Liverpool Daily Post, 5 June, 1986, p.14-15.
Joe Riley, 'Willy's View of Life', Liverpool Echo, 14 July, 1980, p.6.
Nick Smurthwaite, 'Educating Willy', The Guardian, 20 October, 1987, p.13.
Robin Thornber, 'The School in the 'Pool', The Guardian, 6 March, 1979.
Antony Thorncroft, 'One for the Road', Plays and Players, January, 1988, p. 34-5.
Irving Wardle, 'Demolition derby', The Times, 23 October, 1987, p.20.

'Our Day Out' 1977

Anon, 'Willy's day out', Daily Telegraph, 10 February, 1986.
Robert Hewison, 'Crusoes in California', The Sunday Times, 4 September, 1983, p.39.
Irving Wardle, 'Our Day Out', The Times, 31 August, 1983, p.8.
Nick Wood, 'Rejects?', The Times Educational Supplement, 9 December, 1985.

'Stags and Hens' 1978

Erlend Clouston, 'It's all down to Willy's non-lavatorial laugh-in', Liverpool Daily Post, 10 October, 1978, p.6.
Irene McManus, 'Stags and Hens', The Guardian, 30 September, 1982.
Joe Riley, 'Willy's work gets a chain reaction', Liverpool Echo, 5 October, 1978, p.6.
Joe Riley, 'Everyman report: trying hard - but might do better', Liverpool Echo, 12 October, 1978.
Joe Riley, 'Scouse Stags stuck in a rut', Liverpool Echo, 25 September, 1986, p.2.

'Daughters of Albion' 1979

Anon., 'Truth within the badinage', The Stage, 10 May, 1979.
Nancy Banks-Smith, 'Daughters of Albion', The Guardian, 2 May, 1979.

'The Boy with the Transistor Radio' 1980

David Self, 'Turning on', The Times Educational Supplement, 14 October, 1988, p.55.

'Educating Rita' 1980

Michael Billington, 'Educating Rita', The Guardian, 17 June, 1986.

Rita Mae Brown, Rubyfruit Jungle, Bantam Books, New York 1983.
Ned Chaillet, 'Entertaining evening of sad comedy', The Times, 18 June, 1980.
Peter Chepstow, 'Educating Rita', Severn House, London 1983.
Michael Coveney, 'Educating Rita', Financial Times, 17 June, 1980.
Patrick Ensor, 'What Julie did then', The Guardian, 16 August, 1980.
Alan Franks, 'What Rita lost along with the shampoo and sets', The Times Higher Educational Supplement, 4 July, 1980.
Rowena Goldman, 'Educating Rita', Drama, October, 1980, p.54.
Simon Howard, 'Educating Rita', Plays and Players, June 1980, p.19-20.
Sheila Johnson, 'Educating Rita', Monthly Film Bulletin, May 1983, p.130.
John Peter, 'Willy Russell: in a class of his own', Sunday Times, 22 June, 1980.
Maggie Richards, 'Changed minds, broken hearts', The Times Higher Educational Supplement, 13 February, 1987, p.14.
Joe Riley, 'Willy Russell probes the meaning of life', Liverpool Echo, 6 February, 1981.
Joe Riley, 'Lovely Rita is taking a turn for the better', Liverpool Echo, 24 March, 1983, p.6.
Theresa Sullivan, 'Educating Rita', Willy Russell, 'Pygmalion', Bernard Shaw, Longman Literature Guidelines, Harlow, 1990.

'Blood Brothers' 1983

Timothy Charles, 'On the trail of Willy Russell's "Blood Brothers",' The Stage, 6 January, 1983.
Timothy Charles, 'Willy Russell-The First Ten Years', Drama, Summer 1983, p.20-21.
Clare Colvin, 'Merseyside comes to London again', The Times, 9 April, 1983.
Steve Grant, 'Blood Brothers', Plays and Players, June 1983, p.28-29.
Philip Key, 'Willy, Barbara .. and a cert musical smasher', Liverpool Daily Post, 7 December, 1982, p.15.
Joe Riley, 'Beatles' star faces a new challenge', Liverpool Echo, 22 December, 1982, p.6.
Joe Riley, 'Willy with a song in his art', Liverpool Echo, 6 January, 1983, p.6.
Joe Riley, 'Russell's done it again', Liverpool Echo, 10 January, 1983, p.2.
Robin Thornber, 'Blood Brothers', The Guardian, 5 June, 1985, p.15.
Irving Wardle, 'Twins caught in fatal trap', The Times, 12 January, 1983, p.9.

'One Summer' 1983

Andrew Morgan, 'Row over Willy's back street kids', Liverpool Echo, 4 August, 1983.
Colin Shearman, 'One Summer and the difference it could make', The Guardian, 9 August, 1983.
Roy West, 'TV row over Russell series', Liverpool Echo, 27 June, 1983, p.1.
John Williams, 'Russell pulls out after TV clashes', Liverpool Daily Post, 28 June, 1983.

Anon., 'Profile: Willy Russell, hairdresser turned playwright. Scouse Wit in the West End', The Independent, 23 January, 1988, p.8.

Nick Baker, 'Escape Artist', The Times Educational Supplement, 15 January, 1988, p.32.

Michael Billington, 'A housewife's charter', The Guardian, 23 January, 1988, p.12.

Stella Flint, 'Shirley Valentine', Plays and Players, April, 1986, p.36.

Sarah Gristwood, 'The coming of age of an actress', The Guardian, 13 January, 1988, p.10.

Philip Key, 'Be my Valentine on a wet Tuesday at the Pier Head', Liverpool Daily Post, 23 November, 1988, p.16-17.

Philip Key, 'Broadway loses its heart to Valentine', Liverpool Daily Post, 18 February, 1989, p.13.

Brenda Maddox, 'Shirley Decides She's Had Enough', The New York Times, 12 February, 1989.

Joe Riley, 'Willy rustles up a play for lady Valentine', Liverpool Echo, 12 March, 1986, p.7.

Joe Riley, 'Staggeringly vital performance', Liverpool Echo, 14 March, 1986.

Irving Wardle, 'Scouse mouse breaks out in the Aegean', The Times, 23 January, 1988, p.20.

Ian Williams, 'Russell's road', Plays and Players, October, 1987, p.8-9.